STARS
of the
SCREEN

STARS
of the
SCREEN

**DON MACPHERSON, JULIE WELCH
AND LOUISE BRODY**

PHOTOGRAPHS FROM
THE KOBAL COLLECTION

Conran Octopus

First Published in 1989 by
Conran Octopus Limited
37 Shelton Street
London WC2H 9HN

Acknowledgments The publishers would like to thank the following film distribution and production companies whose film stills and publicity portraits appear in this book: A.F.E., Allied Artists, Anglo Amalgamated, Avco Embassy, CBS Theatrical Films, Cocinor, Columbia Pictures, Constantin, Embassy, EMI, Eon, Europa Film, Gaumont, Janus, Ladd Company, London Films, Long Road, Lucasfilm, Lux, Malpaso, MGM, Mirisch, Mutual, NBC, New World, Orion, Paramount Pictures, Pathé, Produzione Europee Associates, Rank, Rastar, Remus, Republic, RKO, Selznick International, Seven Arts, SNC, Speva, Svenskfilmindustri, Titanus, Tri-Star, 20th Century Fox, United Artists, Universal Pictures, Warner Brothers.

Typeset by SX Composing Limited
Printed and bound in Hong Kong

PAGE 2: Publicity Portrait for *Singin' in the Rain*, 1952

PAGE 6: Louise Brooks, studio portrait, 1928. Photographer Eugene Robert Richee

CONTENTS

THE SILENT ERA

CLARA BOW

Clara Bow was the 'It' girl: a rinky-dink little hotsy with sparkling eyes and a thoroughly modern hair-do, who was billed as 'The Hottest Baby of the Jazz Age'. She started her working life in Brooklyn as a telephone receptionist, but in 1922 at the age of sixteen won a beauty contest which took her to Hollywood. Her prize was a lot of hard work: forty-nine films in eight years.

Bow personified the era's pepped-up infatuation with living for kicks, and in *Daughters of Pleasure*, 1924, *The Plastic Age*, 1925, and *Fascinating Youth*, 1926, she resembled a fluttering moth endlessly drawn to a male light. In *It*, 1927, as a lingerie salesgirl who makes a beeline for her boss, she personified the era's idea of sex appeal; batting her eyelids and flirtatiously glancing back over her shoulder, she became the heroine of America's new class of shopgirls in the big cities. With her flaming red hair, matching limousine and pet dogs, Bow played up to her reputation as a highly-sexed, fun-loving gal, and movies such as *Red Hair*, *Ladies of the Mob*, *The Fleet's In*, *Three Week-Ends*, all 1928, and *The Wild Party*, *Dangerous Curves* and *The Saturday Night Kid*, all 1929, suitably completed the picture.

But Bow's star waned towards the end of the decade. Her honking Brooklyn accent was, on the face of it, no asset when the talkies arrived, but she might yet have survived had not her private life turned sour with a divorce scandal and stories of bad gambling debts. Then in 1930 her secretary revealed to a magazine the secrets of Bow's wild weekends with liquor, drugs and what seemed to be football teams of male admirers. The nervous strain soon showed in a breakdown. After her final film, *Hoopla*, 1933, for Fox, she retired with her husband to Nevada: the 'It' girl had just had enough. The girl they called 'Flaming Youth Personified' had burned out.

ABOVE: *The Wild Party*, 1929, with Fredric March
OPPOSITE: studio portrait, 1926.
Photographer Eugene Robert Richee

RUDOLPH VALENTINO

Sixty years after his death, Valentino's name is still synonymous with steamy foreign passion, and he remains the erotic phenomenon with whom his successors are inevitably compared. But because his acting style, spawned by the demands of silent films, now looks almost farcical we tend to forget the staggering impact he had on his contemporaries. His magnetism lay in his ability to combine high-voltage eroticism with an underlying *politesse*; he might seduce well brought up young ladies in thrillingly unthinkable ways, but the two of them would then live happily ever after. Valentino's quintessential role was as Sheik Ahmed Ben Hassan to Agnes Ayres's Lady Diana in *The Sheik*, a high-romance drama which provided post-war audiences with the perfect paradigm of romantic-sexual escapism. His raw wooing of Lady Diana, half-draped and liquid-eyed, with nostrils open at full throttle, was a star turn which exemplified Valentino's sexual attraction as both predator and haven.

The son of a southern Italian vet, Rudolph Valentino had arrived alone in the USA at the age of eighteen, and then had to serve a long Hollywood apprenticeship playing romantic baddies in a series of unmemorable films before he was launched in 1921 by *The Four Horsemen of the Apocalypse*, one of Metro's biggest ever successes, in which director Rex Ingram cast him as Julio, a debonair wastrel who redeems himself in the First World War. *The Sheik* brought Valentino a passionate female following that has never been equalled, and, for five years, he was the screen's great lover in huge box-office successes like *Blood and Sand*, *The Eagle* and *The Son of the Sheik*, although other pictures such as *Monsieur Beaucaire* and *A Sainted Devil* were more tepidly received, probably because he was playing more effeminate characters.

Equally important for both the studio and his audiences, Valentino's per-

LEFT: publicity portrait for *A Sainted Devil*, 1924

sonal life did not live up to his screen image. His first marriage, to Jean Acker, lasted only one day, while his second wife, Natasha Rambova, henpecked him unmercifully; towards the end of his life, he became an object of heterosexual male contempt, condemned in the press as a Pink Powder Puff. There has been much subsequent speculation about Valentino's sexuality; whether Rambova, for instance, had lesbian traits that brought out the latent homosexuality in her husband, or whether Valentino was a forerunner of the contemporary androgynous male represented by David Bowie and Boy George. As it was, heavily in debt, and with his

LEFT: dancing with Natasha Rambova c. 1924
BELOW: *The Sheik*, 1921, with Agnes Ayres

career past its peak, Valentino succumbed to peritonitis in New York on 23 August 1926, at the age of thirty-one. His tragically early death was thus probably opportune. Thousands of grief-stricken women supplied a legendary funeral extravaganza, and his mythical status was ensured.

RIGHT: *A Sainted Devil*, 1924, with Nita Naldi
BELOW: *Monsieur Beaucaire*, 1924, with André Daven

On screen Mary Pickford was 'Little Mary', 'The Girl with the Golden Curls', the helpless ragdoll Cinderella who never went to the ball. But off screen, this professional innocent took her career very much into her own hands. By 1916 it was said that 'whoever emerged in possession of a contract with Mary Pickford was going to hold the whip hand in the whole industry' Her great achievement was to square the shrewd business woman with her screen persona as a guileless waif in movies such as *Tess of the Storm Country*, 1914, *Cinderella*, 1915, *The Foundling*, 1916, *Poor Little Rich Girl*, 1917, and *Daddy Long Legs*, 1919. She was all of twenty-seven and a multi-millionairess when she played the twelve-year-old orphan *Pollyanna* in 1920, one year after she joined forces with D. W. Griffith, Charlie Chaplin and Douglas Fairbanks Sr to form United Artists. Pickford married her charming Prince Fairbanks, and for a few frenzied years the two inspired adulation from all round the world. Their home, 'Pickfair', became a fairy-tale palace for Hollywood's favourite king and queen.

Pickford's famous golden curls surrounded a face which could look as hard as nails and just as unyielding. She never allowed her pull on an audience's emotions to waver for an instant; audiences returned the compliment by refusing to desert her for over twenty years. Her favoured cameraman Charles Rosher devised lighting techniques which helped her keep as fresh as apple-blossom as she slipped into her thirties. She did play mature roles; but in 1933, with fans clamouring for her to play Heidi, Alice in Wonderland or Cinderella again, she retired. 'I am sick of Cinderella parts, of wearing rags and tatters,' she admitted. 'I want to wear smart clothes and play the lover.'

ABOVE: studio portrait, c. 1918.
  Photographer Nelson Evans
RIGHT: *The Taming of the Shrew*, 1929, with
  Douglas Fairbanks Sr

JOHN GILBERT

Gilbert became Valentino's undisputed successor as the great lover of the silent screen playing leading man to Greta Garbo in *Flesh and the Devil.* It was the start of one of the most romantic on-and-off screen liaisons ever; infatuated, he charmed her and proposed frequently, but she repeatedly turned him down and later denied that they had ever had an affair at all. On the screen he was impetuous and ardent, with a youthful sincerity and dashing smile that distinguished him from the rather more menacing Valentino, and his one imperfection, an awfully big nose, seemed to make him all the more appealing. In many ways he was a forerunner of Gable and Errol Flynn, with his uncomplicated, earthy, masculine energy. Ironically, though, Gilbert is now remembered less for his classic roles in silent films than for the tragic and rapid disintegration of his career at the onset of sound.

The son of a comic author, he used family connections to escape his unglamorous job as a rubber goods salesman, finding work as a bit player while he was still in his late teens. He moved up gradually via various unmemorable movies to steady employment as a leading man with Fox, then embarked on the most highly successful phase of his career with MGM, appearing in a succession of smash hits: *He Who Gets Slapped, The Merry Widow, The Big Parade* and *La Bohème.*

In 1927, Gilbert made his first film with Garbo, *Flesh and the Devil,* followed by *Love,* 1927, and *A Woman of Affairs,* 1929. He was deluged with fan mail and became the constant subject of gossip columns. Already married and divorced, his revenge on Garbo after she rejected him was to get married again, to someone else.

OPPOSITE: studio portrait, c. 1928.
Photographer Ruth Harriet Louise
ABOVE: *Wife of the Centaur,* 1924, with
Aileen Pringle
LEFT: *La Bohème,* 1926, with Lillian Gish

His last silent film, *Desert Nights*, went out in 1929, and after that it was all downhill. His debut in the talkies in the balcony scene from 'Romeo and Juliet' in *The Hollywood Revue* of 1929 was not a success, but the real thumbs-down was given to *His Glorious Night*, for which audience reaction was divided between embarrassed sniggers and outright hilarity. Gilbert's failure was not, contrary to popular misconception, the inevitable result of a high, silly voice; in fact he spoke in a perfectly acceptable light tenor. In reality, it was his inability to master a new and different acting technique, and his increasingly sour personal conflict with Louis B. Mayer, that destroyed his career. He saw out his contract, even made reasonable films, but by then his confidence was in pieces. He had always been a heavy drinker, and in 1936 he drank himself to death.

ABOVE: *Flesh and the Devil*, 1927, with Greta Garbo

When the Paris-made *Madame Sans-Gêne*, 1925, received its New York première in Times Square, Gloria Swanson arrived with a real-life Marquis as her (third) husband to be treated like royalty. Her name was given the largest billing ever seen, spelt out in electric lights along the entire façade of the cinema, with the American flag and French tricolour flapping in the wind. 'I have decided that when I am a star, I will be every inch and every moment the star,' she once said.

Swanson's father was Swedish-Italian, her mother of Polish-French-German stock, and Swanson's looks were thought to combine both waif and vamp-like qualities. After a spell as a 'Sennett Girl', she found her svengali in the young Cecil B. DeMille at Paramount for a series of bold, scandalous, sex-laced movies such as *Male and Female, Don't Change Your Husband*, both 1919, and *Why Change Your Wife?*, 1920. Swanson brought middle America into shocked contact with the roaring twenties. Without inhibition she indulged America's fascination for adultery, luxury, love triangles and female sexual discovery. Swanson mocked the movies' self-imposed moralizing. She glorified in the trappings of sexual fetishes, the satin lingerie, the jewelled headdresses, silk gowns, chiffon hats and expensive furs; and sported a narrow-lipped expression and tight hairstyle that seemed almost matronly.

Swanson was always a gift for Paramount's publicists, who, among other schemes, cooked up a feud between her and rival Pola Negri. But in 1926 she turned down offers of $17,500 a week to make her own movies through United Artists. A dispute between herself and director Erich von Stroheim wrecked their perversely brilliant *Queen Kelly*, 1928, although she recovered from disaster by winning an Oscar nomination for her part as *Sadie Thompson*, 1928.

Swanson made more pictures, but

RIGHT: studio portrait, 1919.
Photographer Nelson Evans

her ascendancy waned with the Depression years, when her wild extravagance and regal persona appeared almost embarrassing. It never stopped her returning in style. When she played the silent star Norma Desmond in Billy Wilder's *Sunset Boulevard*, 1950, she was still only fifty-three, but her era seemed centuries away. 'I am still big,' she says in character. 'It's the pictures that got smaller.' That sad mixture of overblown pride and undeniable truth will remain her epitaph.

RIGHT: studio publicity, c. 1920
BELOW: *Queen Kelly*, 1928, with Walter Byron
OPPOSITE: *The Thief of Bagdad*, 1924, with Julanne Johnston

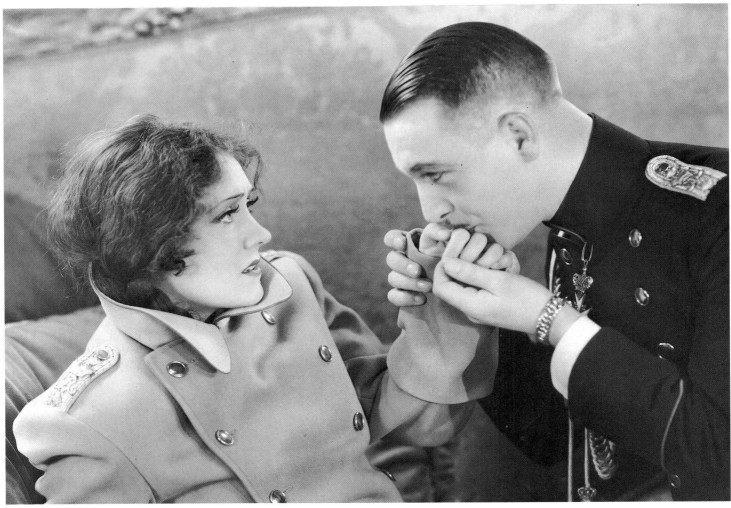

Fairbanks Sr was a perfect piece of human engineering, combining balletic vitality and excellent coordination with heart-stopping good looks: tumbling dark curls, a piratical grin and lots of sexy crinkles around the eyes. He was a considerable athlete and daring gymnast who never proposed to a girl in the ordinary way: his declarations of love or proposals of marriage were always preceded by a string of sword fights, perilous journeys and miraculous feats of mountaineering and horsemanship. He was also always terribly honourable about it, as in *The Thief of Bagdad* when he steals into the princess' bedroom with the confidence of a cat-burglar and the respectability of a vicar.

Fairbanks Sr's screen persona was that of the dashing, unpretentious, lovable young blade who had no hang-ups about anything — the complete antithesis of Valentino although, like him, he was in the fancy-dress trade, buccaneering his way through films like *Robin Hood*, *The Gaucho* and *The Iron Mask* in a magnificent selection of breeches, harem pants, thigh boots, buckles, belts and wide-brimmed hats. His swashbuckling epics fuelled the American need for romance and adventure and the appeal of his fantasy escapism was vast, not only to women, who longed to be rescued by him, but also to boys and men, who admired his aura of frolicsome good health and clean-living mischievousness. Valentino would have taken advantage of a girl; Doug's whole persona was wrapped about the fact he would not. Even fathers would have been content to let their daughters leave the house with him at night. His success and popularity on screen was made more heady by his romance with Mary Pickford, America's Little Sweetheart, and despite the fact that they both had to ditch their respective spouses in order to marry in 1920, their popularity was heightened rather than

ABOVE: *The Three Musketeers*, 1921, with Barbara La Marr
RIGHT: *The Black Pirate*, 1926

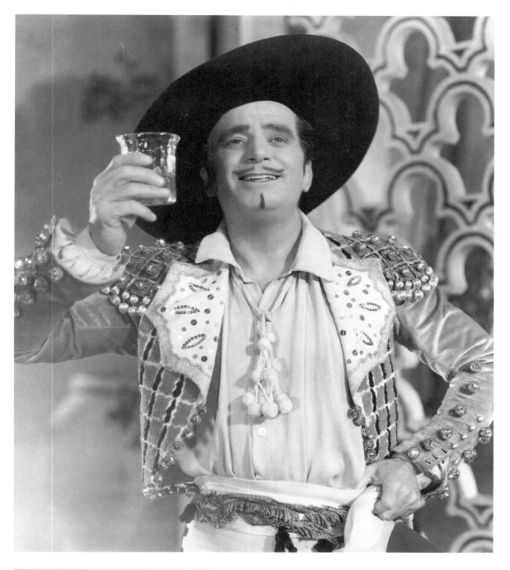

tarnished by the union. Thousands of adoring fans made their European honeymoon resemble a royal procession, and they went on to become the First Family of Hollywood.

Fairbanks himself had had a fairly unconventional family life. The youngest of three sons, who were all devoted to their mother, a Southern beauty who had been married three times, he lacked a father figure on whom to model himself, which perhaps explains why he retained the persona of a boy well into adult life. The family was a very close one and both John and Robert, his two elder brothers, later worked in Doug's film empire.

Young Fairbanks capitalized on his childhood passion for acting after unsuccessful spells at Harvard — where he seems to have spent most of his time in the gymnasium — and on Wall Street. In 1915, he went West to make acrobatic dramas for the Triangle Film Company, earning $2,000 a week, before he moved on to his heroic parts in swashbuckling epics in the early twenties: a swordsman in *The Mark of Zorro*, D'Artagnan in *The Three Musketeers*, the outlawed Earl of Huntingdon in *Robin Hood*, and the prince of thieves in *The Thief of Bagdad*.

By the time sound came Fairbanks was in his forties and, although there was nothing wrong with his speaking voice, he was too firmly rooted in his era to adapt to the change of techniques required. By 1934 his marriage with Mary Pickford was over and he retired; only five years later he died of a heart attack. His films have endured as achievements of athletic imagination that can stand alongside modern equivalents like the ice dancing of Torvill and Dean and, despite the fancy dress, they can be viewed without hilarity or incredulity.

ABOVE: *The Private Life of Don Juan*, 1934
LEFT: *Don Q Son of Zorro*, 1925, with Mary Astor

21

LILLIAN GISH

The Gish sisters were complementary and exceptionally hard-working actresses, learning their craft through exacting schedules and changing parts two or three times a week. Of the two, Dorothy was the slighter actress, a younger echo of Lillian, though both possessed that wispy frailty and freshness which was to prove so appealing. Dorothy kept up a long and successful film and stage career, but she was always eclipsed by her more ethereal sister and it is Lillian's name that appears under 'Gish' in the annals of cinema history.

Lillian is unjustly recognized as the paragon of simple, old-fashioned, nineteenth-century feminine virtue. D. W. Griffith saw her as a virgin of true heart, self-sacrificing and rather unexciting; and certainly her roles in *Hearts of the World*, 1918, *Broken Blossoms*,

True Heart Susie, both 1919, and *Orphans of the Storm*, 1921, are saturated with Griffith's brand of unctuous Victorian sentimentality. But the role which brought Gish worldwide fame — Elsie Stoneman in *Birth of a Nation*, 1915 — already seemed to speak of a bygone age.

For Lillian Gish was truly the first *modern* actress in cinema. Audiences loved her ability to suggest complex emotions directly to the camera. Here, for the first time, was an actress who was not merely untheatrical but positively cinematic. In some of the earliest close-ups she manages to project all the contradictions of a Pre-Raphaelite painting. Garlanded, virginal, she is also highly sensual, and she could suggest a devastating mix of vulnerable innocence and underlying passion. As a gentle Virginian girl who

murders an assailant in *The Wind*, 1928, Gish conveys emotions of fear and devotion as if for the first time, her face at once terrifying and exhilarating.

Contracted to MGM in 1925 for $8,000 a week, Gish made a series of fine pictures but fell foul of a studio publicity machine which saw her as overpaid and out of fashion. In Louise Brooks' words, she was 'stigmatized at the age of thirty-one as a grasping, silly, sexless antique', but after her departure from Hollywood in the late twenties, she maintained a highly successful stage career, punctuated by occasional character parts in cinema and television.

OPPOSITE: *The Wind*, 1928
ABOVE: *Orphans of the Storm*, 1921, with Dorothy Gish

JOHN BARRYMORE

One of the great tragi-romantic heroes of the silents in his heyday, Barrymore had a playful and ebullient screen personality, but also a self-destruct mechanism which had started with heavy drinking in his teens and ultimately drove him to the alcoholics' clinic. His stunningly patrician good looks gave him his nickname, the Great Profile, and he lived out his role as a dedicated ladies' man off stage, getting through four wives and numerous scandalous liaisons.

Barrymore came from a strong theatrical background. His father, who came from an English upper crust background, had appalled his family by going on the stage, and his mother was the actress Georgiana Drew. Her death, when John was only ten, devastated him and by the time he was fifteen he was already becoming dependent on alcohol. Although he started out working as a cartoonist, he followed family tradition and went on the Broadway stage in 1903. Barrymore built up a reputation as one of the most admired stage actors of his day and maintained a flourishing theatrical career for years after he had successfully moved into films. He achieved international stardom in 1920 with *Dr Jekyll and Mr Hyde*, and in 1924 made *Beau Brummel* opposite Mary Astor, who was then aged only seventeen. They embarked on a passionate romance, but two years later he fell in love with nineteen-year-old Dolores Costello, his leading lady in *The Sea Beast*, 1926, the screen adaptation of Melville's novel, 'Moby Dick'. He dropped Mary Astor and, at the age of forty-five, made Costello his third wife.

Not unexpectedly, Barrymore adapted to the talkies with effortless success, making his debut in *The Show of Shows* in 1929. His stage work now proved invaluable experience and the early thirties were a good time for him; in *Grand Hotel*, 1932, he played opposite Garbo, who later commented that Barrymore had the 'divine mad-

LEFT: publicity portrait for *Grand Hotel*, 1932

ness' of all great artists. But his drinking was increasingly causing problems. He now needed cue cards to remember his lines and after completing *Romeo and Juliet* he packed himself off to a clinic to dry out. His last years were beset by financial troubles which no doubt prompted his return to the stage where he acted, and fell down, in some very bad plays before he died of pneumonia in 1942.

LEFT: *Tempest*, 1928, with Camilla Horn
BELOW: *Eternal Love*, 1929, with Camilla Horn

RIGHT: *Grand Hotel*, 1932, with Greta Garbo
BELOW: *Twentieth Century*, 1934, with
    Carole Lombard

When Louise Brooks was working as a shopgirl in Macy's in her mid-forties she was almost forgotten. Hollywood had shunned her, her movies were no longer shown, her name was a dim footnote in the film histories. But as other stars dimmed, her reputation grew. 'There is no Garbo', exclaimed Henri Langlois in the 1950s, 'only Louise Brooks.' To look at her early photos, all bobbed hair and flapper costumes, she seems a typical jazz baby of the 1920s. But not only did she possess an incandescent beauty and smile which appealed to both men and women, she also projected a peculiarly bewitching, pleasure-seeking aura.

At a time when many screen actresses were still hidebound by stilted stage techniques, Brooks incarnated a personality which was lively, magnetic and directly erotic. She had started out as a Ziegfeld showgirl, before getting roles in run of the mill pictures like *Just Another Blonde*, 1926, and *Rolled Stockings*, 1927, for Paramount. The next year she shone in a better part in Howard Hawks' *A Girl in Every Port*, and opposite Richard Arlen in Wellman's *Beggars of Life*, 1928, in which she brought a recognizably modern, androgynous quality to her role as a woman dressed as a man on the run on the freight trains. The German film director G.W. Pabst was so impressed by this twenty-three-year-old Kansas girl that he offered her the leading role as Lulu in an adaptation of Wedekind's plays, and Brooks packed her bags for Berlin. The change of scene worked wonders: 'I would be treated by Pabst with a kind of decency and respect unknown to me in Hollywood,' she later wrote. In *Die Büchse der Pandora/Pandora's Box*, 1929, she played a *femme fatale* living in a world of sexual pleasure. Brooks created a heroine who was intensely alive and tragic, an innocent who is yet a flirtatiously provocative symbol of amoral hedonism that fits exactly with our

RIGHT: studio portrait, c. 1928.
Photographer Eugene Robert Richee

modern interpretation of those times. Despite her two European successes – *Das Tagebuch einer Verlorenen/Diary of a Lost Girl*, also directed by Pabst, was released in the same year as *Pandora's Box* – Brooks returned to Hollywood. But she was unwilling to bow down to dictates which she considered banal. She resisted unsuitable parts (such as the Harlow role in *The Public Enemy*), but was gradually crushed: in punishment for her disobedience, she was forced into accepting ever smaller roles. She scathingly described that dispiriting period of her career in a series of essays which she published from the fifties, long after she had abandoned her acting career and started to develop her capacity for articulate and penetrating film criticism.

Unsubdued by the Hollywood system, but ultimately defeated by it, Brooks, like Garbo, possessed a defiant pride and rebellious strength that has increased her standing over the years, the more so as general cynicism about the reality of 'Hollywood' has grown. Perhaps she herself came closest to defining her peculiar cinematic power when she wrote: 'The art of films does not consist of descriptive movement of face and body, but in the movements of thought and soul, transmitted in a kind of intense isolation.'

ABOVE: publicity portrait for *The Canary Murder Case*, 1929
LEFT: publicity portrait for *Beggars of Life* 1928, with Richard Arlen. Photographer Otto Dyar

Theda Bara appeared like a thunderbolt in a world where marriage was an inviolate sanctuary, and the relationship between husbands and wives supposed to be sober and straitlaced. With her dark, flashing eyes and flowing hair, she was a compelling choice for the screen's first 'vamp': a threatening, other-worldly figure robed in muslin, jewels and feathers, who would toss back her head and laugh at her unfortunate lover's destruction. Her first starring role, *A Fool There Was*, 1915, was a heady brew of sinful melodrama concocted by the young William Fox. It set this twenty-five-year-old actress firmly in the American public's fevered imagination as a mysterious she-devil, while Fox's razzamatazz proclaimed her to be the offspring of a sheik and a princess, her name an anagram of ARAB DEATH.

She was like a living illustration of 'Sin' from a child's Bible picture-book, and she appealed to a growing middle-class audience for whom the sophistications of the love triangle were of enormous interest. In more than thirty-five films made over five years, Bara played Salome, Camille, Madame Du Barry and Cleopatra, creating a repertoire of archetypal temptresses copied by succeeding generations. Bara's image was the evil and erotic 'Dark Angel of Destiny', hair falling languorously over bare shoulders, breasts cupped by gilded serpents. It seemed to matter little that in reality the heroine of *Tiger Woman*, *Purgatory*, *Eternal Sin* and *Sin*, all 1914-1919, was a tailor's daughter from Ohio, christened Theodosia Goodman.

By 1919 the vogue for man-eating vampires was over. Fox, his company now firmly established thanks to Bara, had no more use for her. She was left as an almost unemployable legend, the first leading lady offered up on a plate for her sexual allure and then callously discarded.

ABOVE: publicity portrait for *Cleopatra*, 1917.
  Photographer Witzel

OVER: Marlene Dietrich, studio portrait, 1935.
  Photographer Eugene Robert Richee

THE STUDIO YEARS

WILLIAM POWELL

William Powell's urbane and not-quite-decent image was enhanced by a pair of sensually droopy eyelids, underneath which his eyes would rove knowingly around the more interesting points of his leading ladies. In the thirties he won extraordinary popularity in *The Thin Man* series, playing one half of the much-loved husband-and-wife team, Nick and Nora Charles, Dashiell Hammett's sophisticated sleuths who were never short of a good line or the ice for their dry martinis. His persona shifted interestingly over his career, from his days of silent villains to Nora Charles's rather thrilling husband, and on to the irascible but kind-hearted father figure he played in *Life with Father*, towards the end of his career.

Powell played numerous baddies in the silent era, but his career only really took off with the arrival of sound, when he emerged as a skilled comedy actor who played well-mannered and fun-loving, but nevertheless slightly caddish, good guys — the type who would lead girls astray. He was amusing, glossy, sophisticated, sour, the personification of the best of thirties comedy. He and Loy teamed up with Spencer Tracy and Jean Harlow in *Libeled Lady*, 1936, a perfect vehicle for Powell's air of worldly *savoir-faire*, and he also played suave professional men turned sleuths again opposite Ginger Rogers in *Star of Midnight*, 1935, and Jean Arthur in *The Ex-Mrs Bradford*, 1936. His biggest acting success was as yet to come, however, playing the husband of Irene Dunne in *Life with Father*, for which he won an Academy Award nomination in 1947. As he grew old he moved on to character parts, and retired in 1955 after making his 95th film.

OPPOSITE: studio portrait, c. 1930
ABOVE: on set for *Reckless*, 1935, with
    Jean Harlow
LEFT: *Libeled Lady*, 1936, with Myrna Loy

RONALD COLMAN

Reserved and courteous, hands characteristically tucked in his pockets, Ronald Colman was British in the most charming way, projecting reliability without stuffiness and good manners without insincerity. Women found his wistful, faraway look – hinting at past tragedies bravely borne – and his dashing looks quite irresistible. In one of his most powerful performances as the nobly self-sacrificing Sidney Carton in *A Tale of Two Cities*, 1935, he forbore to declare his love for Elizabeth Allan, but typically did the 'far, far better thing' and died for her sake. It seemed entirely in character when, in the early thirties, he departed for 20th Century Fox after Sam Goldwyn opined that his acting would be all the better for a few drinks inside him.

Born in England and married to British actress Benita Hume, Colman never lost his European charm even though he settled and spent most of his working life in the USA. He established himself as a romantic hero of the silents and after getting his break opposite Lillian Gish in *The White Sister*, 1923, he and Vilma Banky became one of the great teams of the period in screen romances like *The Magic Flame*, 1927, and *Two Lovers*, 1928. His first major sound success was *Bulldog Drummond* in 1929 and his subsequent films were invariably suited to his aura of gentlemanly refinement, as in *Arrowsmith*, *The Masquerader*, *Bulldog Drummond Strikes Back* and *The Man Who Broke the Bank at Monte Carlo*.

Blessed with a gorgeous speaking voice, the witty and urbane Colman went on to become even more popular after the advent of sound. He adapted quickly to the restraint and understatement required, but he had to wait another twenty years for the industry's top prize, finally winning an Oscar towards the end of his career as the

ABOVE: studio portrait, c. 1929
RIGHT: *The Prisoner of Zenda*, 1937, with Madeleine Carroll
OPPOSITE: *The Magic Flame*, 1927, with Vilma Banky

deluded Shakespearian actor in *A Double Life*, 1947. By then he had shown his range in a wide number of roles stretching from adventure heroes, as the eponymous empire-builder *Clive of India*, 1935, and the lead in *The Prisoner of Zenda*, 1937, to well-connected rogues like the lead in *Raffles*, 1930, which he played with great flair. Age only served to increase his tweedy attractiveness, as in *Random Harvest* opposite Greer Garson, and his appeal to women remained undiminished when he retired in his early sixties.

RIGHT: studio portrait, 1939.
        Photographer Eugene Richee
BELOW: *Random Harvest*, 1942, with
        Greer Garson

CAROLE LOMBARD

When she died in a plane crash in 1942, aged only thirty-four, Carole Lombard was already a favourite with the American public and known as one of its finest comediennes. As Mrs Clark Gable, she was also one half of show business' most glamorous couple. She had spent the twenties playing in routine movies for more than one studio, but from the time she found her true form in *Twentieth Century*, 1934, Lombard became a prime example of how swiftly the studio system could exploit and promote a rising star and yet produce dynamic results.

In a favourite train compartment scene in *Twentieth Century*, Lombard shouts, yelps, stamps her feet, curses and storms against the wily John Barrymore, who plays an outrageously ham actor–manager. She is petite, wiry, glamorous; he is gargantuan, like a comic gargoyle. As she persists in defying him, the scene mounts to fever pitch, with Lombard controlling the ricocheting dialogue of Ben Hecht and Charles MacArthur in double-quick time. With this film she became a top-rank star, and set the standard for the screwball comedies of the next decade. For before this, such rebellious female behaviour would have been frowned upon, acceptable only in the topsy-turvy world of the anarchic Mack Sennett comedies in which Lombard had herself spent two years in 1927–8. Now she stamped an identity on her era, and turned that brand of disruptive, manic energy into a positive quality: 'wackiness'. In *My Man Godfrey*, 1936, *Nothing Sacred*, 1937, and her crowning glory *To Be Or Not To Be*, 1942, Lombard waged good-natured war against middle-class restraint, conventions and conformity.

In *My Man Godfrey*, Lombard is the spoiled little rich girl who chases after the new butler (William Powell – in real life her husband from 1931 to 1933). Her celebration of a woman's need to

LEFT: studio portrait, 1932.
Photographer Eugene Robert Richee

satisfy her desires is symptomatic of the new climate of female self-confidence, and only in such an atmosphere could Lombard have expressed such bemused bewilderment at the idea of *not* satisfying the pleasure principle. It was a performance that won her the only Oscar nomination of her career. In *Nothing Sacred* Lombard is the pivot around which a bitter satire turns. She plays a young girl who becomes headline news when it is found she is dying of radium poisoning. Such a gift for black comedy was rare in Hollywood stars, but Lombard's role

LEFT: off set *The Princess Comes Across*, 1936.
Photographer Don English
BELOW: publicity portrait for *The Gay Bride*, 1934, with Chester Morris.
Photographer Clarence Sinclair Bull

in Ernst Lubitsch's satire, *To Be Or Not To Be*, showed her to be a master of it, ensnared in a farce of Warsaw actors impersonating wartime Nazis. It was her last film. But it underlined the fact that Lombard had brought Hollywood a new sophistication without losing the rough and ready, small-town attitudes upon which both she and the famous film capital thrived.

RIGHT: studio portrait, 1936.
 Photographer William Walling Jr
BELOW: studio publicity, c. 1937, with
 Clark Gable

HENRY FONDA

One of Hollywood's most earnest heroes, Fonda had a chiselled sobriety perfectly suited to the noble idealism of his roles as representative of the national spirit and conscience. His great Americans, whether military, Western or political, struggled against anarchy and disorder. He played a youthfully solemn Abe Lincoln in John Ford's *Young Mr Lincoln*, 1939, the strong-minded symbol of frontier justice, Wyatt Earp in *My Darling Clementine*, and Tom Joad in *The Grapes of Wrath*, a key film of conscience. It was perhaps appropriate that in the sixties, when the USA had lost its innocence, the most important symbol of its goodness played a vicious sadist, in *Once Upon A Time In The West*, 1968.

Fonda's gift for conveying noble idealism and human unworthiness at the same time made him equally strong in more equivocal roles, playing men who had the courage to attempt heroic tasks without necessarily being up to them. He could be angry or confused without compromising his virility: his voice, with its homely Nebraska twang, cracked with honest, manly emotion when he was overwhelmed with feeling. Fonda very rarely got caught in a clinch and when he kissed, it was usually the official married peck. Marriage for him was usually a duty or a cerebral affair, though the closing wedding scene in *My Darling Clementine* was one of the most moving images ever of marriage and stability taming the Wild West.

Fonda appeared frequently on the Broadway stage and, at the age of seventy-three, was an enormous success in a one-man show as the famous liberal lawyer, Clarence Darrow. He died only a year after winning an Oscar for his performance in *On Golden Pond*, as the irascible but still bravely unbowed father.

OPPOSITE: studio portrait, c. 1936
ABOVE: publicity portrait for *My Darling Clementine*, 1946
LEFT: *That Certain Woman*, 1937, with Bette Davis

41

JAMES CAGNEY

From the moment Cagney shoved half a grapefruit into Mae Clarke's face in *The Public Enemy*, 1931, his ebullient delinquency was irresistible. He was the quintessential gangster of the cinema; a cruel hoodlum with a disturbing childlike look and an inimitable staccato style of speech fired off like the emptying of a machine gun who went around wrecking speakeasies, breaking out of jail, roughing up women and generally behaving very badly indeed.

But under the tough exterior was an underlying vulnerability which surfaced in the desire to be mothered or to set a good example, as in his gangster role in *Angels With Dirty Faces*, 1938. His appeal lay in the idea that under the gangster there lurked a vulnerable kid: in *White Heat*, 1949, he delivered a telling farewell to the world, crying 'Top of the world, Ma!', discharging his gun into a gas tank and blowing himself to eternity.

Cagney's childhood background was as formatively rough as that of any of his characters. Born in Manhattan's Lower East Side in 1899, he established an early reputation for tough street fighting and at one time aspired to a boxing career, but in fact entered show business as a vaudeville dancer in drag. His fifth film, *The Public Enemy*, made him a star and he carried through the gangster persona in films like *Lady Killer*, 1933, and *The Roaring Twenties*, 1939, to become one of the top ten box-office draws. Underlying the persona was a neurotic sexuality, nervy and jumpy, which became positively psychotic in *White Heat*, bridging the gap between thirties tough guy and fifties neurotic hero.

Having retired in 1961, he emerged over twenty years later to play the police chief in *Ragtime*.

ABOVE: *The Public Enemy*, 1931, with Jean Harlow
RIGHT: *Picture Snatcher*, 1933, with Alice White
OPPOSITE: studio portrait, c. 1936

GRETA GARBO

Garbo was not always considered the unique and irreplaceable star she seems today. In the mid-1920s, when she was first brought to Hollywood by MGM as the protégé of Swedish director Mauritz Stiller, she was considered an exotic leading lady in the neurotically sensitive tradition of Gloria Swanson or Pola Negri. But in contrast to their overwrought artifice, Garbo brought something new from her Swedish background: simplicity, realism and sincerity. Alone among her contemporaries, she intuitively grasped that the great thrill of cinema was to share a moment of private

OPPOSITE: studio portrait, 1931.
          Photographer Clarence Sinclair Bull
LEFT: *Love*, 1927, with John Gilbert
BELOW: *The Single Standard*, 1929, with
          Nils Asther

revelation with an audience, and this at a time in movie history when, in the words of Roland Barthes, 'capturing the human face still plunged audiences into the deepest ecstasy'.

Garbo was born Greta Louisa Gustafsson, the daughter of a Stockholm labourer. At sixteen she was already playing bit-parts in movies, and by twenty she had attracted the attention of Stiller. He changed her name and put her into *Gösta Berlings Saga*, 1924, which won critical acclaim in Europe. It was only by virtue of Stiller's new contract with MGM, which had as one of its conditions that Garbo should also be put on the payroll, that this diffident star arrived in Hollywood. The reluctant studio had little idea of how to use her. They tried all the usual publicity gambits — posing her with animals, in swimsuits, or even as a healthy athlete testing her biceps — without success. Fortunately her early rebellion against this crude pigeonholing coincided with rapturous acclaim for her American debut in *The Torrent*, 1926. Her insistent reticence was turned to advantage by MGM, who promoted her as a reclusive mystery. Thus was born one of this century's great legends.

She resembled an ethereal vamp in her forcefully erotic silent movies with John Gilbert — *Love* and *Flesh and the Devil*, both 1927, and *A Woman of Affairs*, 1929. If her attitude to love in these films seems blasé, her appreciation of its responsibilities is profound. She is at once fickle and severe, projecting such contradictions with tragic appeal. From the moment when she uttered her first line of dialogue in *Anna Christie*, 1930, she became MGM's leading light: more noble than Shearer, more classy than Harlow, more discreet than Crawford.

Garbo's first classic role was as *Queen Christina*, 1933. In that film her face resembles a mask of alabaster, a blank page upon which audiences

OPPOSITE: publicity portrait for *Romance*, 1930. Photographer George Hurrell
ABOVE: *Mata Hari*, 1931, with Ramon Novarro
LEFT: *Grand Hotel*, 1932, with John Barrymore

could inscribe all manner of emotion and heartbreak. This was subtle and intelligent direction by Rouben Mamoulian, in a style Garbo was to make her own. With title roles as *Anna Karenina*, 1935, and *Camille*, 1936, she perfected the role of the distraught lover. Another elaborate costume drama, *Conquest*, 1937, developed that persona, as Maria Walewska to Charles Boyer's Napoleon, but by now her popularity was greater outside the USA. *Ninotchka*, 1939, advertised as the movie in which 'Garbo laughs', allowed her a change of image, but MGM remained unsympathetic to a star who had always refused to toe the line, and after *Two-Faced Woman*, 1941, Garbo went into a temporary retirement that became permanent.

Her disappearance from the screen paradoxically increased her stature, and made real the hyperbole of MGM publicity. She had brought cinema itself to maturity by yoking the silents' sense of gesture and drama to the realism of the talkies, but remained an enigmatic and unreachable phenomenon. Just look at Garbo's face. Sometimes her strong bones and arched eyebrows are only just visible; the eyes are shaded beneath long lashes that cast shadows on her skin; her hair crowns her forehead and her lips are concealed as if they hold secrets waiting to be revealed. She seems to wish she were invisible: it is not so much a face as a shadow of one, suggested by isolated glimpses and memories, inscrutable and austere. In such a style, she exercised dominion over the earliest secrets of cinema.

LEFT: *Camille*, 1936, with Robert Taylor
OPPOSITE: studio portrait, c. 1929.
Photographer Eugene Richee

Diffident without being timid, and tough but not insensitive, the taciturn Cooper symbolized a new kind of hero, courageous in spirit as well as body. A natural actor whose success lay in the force of his uncomplicated screen persona and his extraordinary power of self-projection, Cooper's most out-standing performance came towards the end of his career in the classic Western, *High Noon*, playing Will Kane, the town marshal left by his friends and allies to stand alone in the showdown against the avenging mob. The man who once described himself as 'just an average guy from the middle of America' had by then come to be much more than that. His refusal to fight or think dirty, and his hard-won triumphs over corruption as a plain country boy who knows what's right, had come to personify the values of middle America and helped to define the Western hero ethic.

Cooper's effect on women was devastating: he had a lanky, hollow-cheeked beauty, which gave the impression that he needed feeding up a bit, and a slow style of movement which was powerfully attractive. His shy, charming and unflappable strength made women feel safe. But it was not quite that simple: Cooper also perfectly captured the American mood. The wholesome gallantry he exuded made women feel slightly ashamed of the way they had carried on over Valentino, Novarro and the other heavy-breathing Latins, and want to redeem themselves with a nice man whose stumbling sincerity could overawe sophisticated women like Carole Lombard in *I Take This Woman*, 1931, Claudette Colbert in *His Woman*, 1931, and Tallulah Bankhead in *Devil and the Deep*, 1932. At the same time, having established himself as a Western hero in *The Virginian*, 1929, Cooper proved that his

ABOVE: *Half a Bride*, 1928, with Esther Ralston
LEFT: *A Farewell to Arms*, 1932, with
  Helen Hayes

masculine qualities and strong aura of honesty were equally appealing to men.

Ironically, Cooper was British. His immigrant father, a judge who owned a ranch in Montana, earned enough to send young Frank – the 'Gary' came later – to England for a private school education, and Cooper kept a trace of the accent as a subtle clipping of his famous soft-spoken drawl. Cooper's private school period was indirectly beneficial in another way: his hip was damaged in a car accident and his long convalescence in Montana, during which he spent as much time as possible on horseback for his hip,

RIGHT: studio portrait, c. 1935.
Photographer Eugene Richee
BELOW: *Morocco*, 1930, with Marlene Dietrich

turned him into an excellent rider.

In fact, he began his film career as an extra in Westerns, falling off horses at $5 a time. By 1927 he was on contract to Paramount, where he won a minor role in *It*, and, just as significantly, the attention of Clara Bow. Although his off-screen romance with her did not last long, it launched him as a heart-throb and perfectly complemented his roles in a string of action pictures. Over the next few years, Cooper had several other well-publicized romances, including a turbulent relationship with Lupe Velez, his leading lady in *Wolf Song*, 1929. His reputation was that of the super virile stud of whom a friend

LEFT: portrait, c. 1936
BELOW: *Today We Live*, 1933, with Joan Crawford
OPPOSITE: studio portrait, 1932.
Photographer Clarence Sinclair Bull

once said, 'He was the greatest cocks-man who ever lived'. However, in 1933 he married a New York socialite, Veronica 'Rocky' Balfe, who turned a blind eye to her husband's subsequent entanglements with his leading ladies such as Marlene Dietrich and Ingrid Bergman. Their life-long union was threatened only once, by Cooper's love affair with an actress, Patricia Neal, when he was fifty and she was twenty-six.

By the end of the thirties, Cooper had risen to become the highest wage-earner in the United States and one of Hollywood's most powerful box-office draws. He reached the top, and stayed there, thanks to an output of consist-ently good films. Although he never troubled himself with more equivocal roles, he was both versatile and flex-ible within self-imposed limits, and he never parodied himself.

In *The Plainsman*, 1936, and *The Westerner*, 1940, his strength and simplicity perfectly suited the arche-typal Western hero, but he could also convey the melancholy detachment of a Hemingway hero in *A Farewell to Arms*, 1932. He turned in a skilled comic performance in *Mr Deeds Goes to Town*, 1936, the Frank Capra movie which put Cooper into American icon-ography for keeps as the man of humanism and virtue triumphing over the forces of violence and corruption. 'To get folks to like you,' he once said, 'I figured you had to sort of be their ideal. I don't mean a handsome knight riding a white horse, but a fellow who answered the description of a right guy.' He may have been unlucky when Goldwyn refused to loan him out for the part of Rhett Butler in *Gone with the Wind*, but his performance in *Sergeant York*, 1941, as a mumbling Tennessee boy who turns from paci-fism to war gallantry, won him his first Oscar. Cooper, in short, could per-

ABOVE: *Beau Geste*, 1939, with Ray Milland
RIGHT: *One Sunday Afternoon*, 1933, with Fay Wray

sonify many facets of America's vision of itself and he was used by an incredible variety of directors – Capra, Hawks, von Sternberg, Wyler, Lubitsch, Vidor and Mann among them.

Though Cooper's first forays into romantic movies were less than successful – as Paramount's 'glorious young lovers', he and Fay Wray never really clicked – he overcame his initial woodenness to star with a wide range of leading ladies, from Marlene Dietrich in *Morocco*, 1930, to Joan Crawford in *Today We Live*, 1933, and ten years later he was nominated for an Oscar with Ingrid Bergman for their chemistry in *For Whom the Bell Tolls*, one of the greatest romantic movies to come out of Hollywood. They played together again in *Saratoga Trunk*, by which time Cooper had matured to an attractive cragginess.

The post-war years were less easy for Cooper. His films were variable in quality and his autumn-to-spring affair with Patricia Neal brought a four-year separation in his marriage. But in 1952 came *High Noon*, in which he stood as the embodiment of moral as well as physical courage. The control, determination and subtlety of his performance won him his second Academy Award. It was not his last Oscar; in April 1961, when he was dying of cancer, he was honoured by the film industry with a Special Academy Award for outstanding services. Less than a month later, he was dead.

ABOVE: *Saratoga Trunk*, 1945, with
     Ingrid Bergman
LEFT: *Mr Deeds Goes to Town*, 1936, with
     Jean Arthur

MAE WEST

Dressed like an inflatable Venus in feathers and pearls, Mae West combined the wit of Oscar Wilde, the roguery of W.C. Fields, and the allure of a bar-room Salome in a style which meant only one thing to most audiences: 'Sex'. That was the title of the 1926 revue that West wrote, directed and produced, and which earned her a jail sentence for obscenity. The daughter of a boxer, West made her first appearance on the stage aged five, and became 'The Baby Vamp'. Movies didn't discover her until she was forty, when she made her film and screenwriting debut with *Night After Night*, 1932. She was as good a reason as any for inventing the talkies, and with *She Done Him Wrong* and *I'm No Angel*, both 1933 and with Cary Grant, and with *Belle of the Nineties*, 1934, she set up a run of hits which made her one of the richest women in America. She revolutionized public acceptance of sexual matters with a constant stream of witty dialogue, innuendo and single-*entendres*, most of which she wrote herself. Despite a backlash from censors in the mid-thirties, she persevered in *Go West Young Man*, 1936, *Every Day's a Holiday*, 1937, and with her peer W. C. Fields in *My Little Chickadee*, 1940; but as the decade ended she returned to Broadway and the international nightclub circuit as a legend in her own lifetime. The disaster of *Myra Breckinridge*, 1970, could not diminish her popularity, nor could her appearance as an eighty-five-year-old vamp in the lamentable *Sextette*, 1978. When she died in 1980 she was mourned by more than the drag queens who had borrowed her style. Immortal lines like 'Come up and see me sometime', and 'Peel me a grape' are still quoted in affectionate parody more than half a century after she first spoke them; not many scriptwriters can boast as much.

LEFT: publicity portrait for *I'm No Angel*, 1933.
Photographer Don English
OPPOSITE: studio portrait, 1938.
Photographer Eugene Robert Richee

DOUGLAS FAIRBANKS Jr

The studios didn't have to look far for a Douglas Fairbanks Sr clone; they had Doug Jr, the son from his first marriage to Anna Beth Sully. American by birth and British by culture, Doug Jr gravitated towards Hollywood in the silent era against his father's wishes, but made little headway until the advent of sound, when he succeeded to his father's buccaneering persona and swashbuckling role despite evidence that his glossy charm was more suited to drawing-room roles. He produced a notable performance as the caddish soldier of fortune, Rupert of Hentzau, in John Cromwell's version of *The Prisoner of Zenda*, 1937, and was one of three soldier pals (Cary Grant and Victor McLaglen were the others) holding the fort – and Joan Fontaine – in the British imperialist yarn, *Gunga Din*.

A well-known socialite, married first to Joan Crawford, Fairbanks Jr was also repeatedly cast in more debonair parts, playing the carefree admirer of Irene Dunne in *Joy of Living*, the student holiday-camp worker amongst man-crazy girls in *Having Wonderful Time*, opposite Ginger Rogers, and with Danielle Darrieux in *The Rage of Paris*, all in 1938. In the forties, he appeared in a series of acclaimed adventure yarns like *Sinbad The Sailor*, 1947, but somehow, perhaps because he was neither wholly British nor wholly American, Doug seemed permanently out of tune with the times. At the start of the fifties he retired from film-making to produce and sometimes play in the television series, 'Douglas Fairbanks Presents'.

LEFT: *Gunga Din*, 1939, with Joan Fontaine
OPPOSITE: studio portrait, 1936.
Photographer Ted Allen

Stewart's romantic strength lay partly in his own amiability and partly in his air of fetching clumsiness: his trousers were unable to stay put over his socks, his gloves would refuse to stop twitching and his hats had a tendency to flip sideways in the presence of young ladies. In *Mr Smith Goes To Washington*, his hat fell off altogether when he met his rival's beautiful daughter. His stooping gawkiness made him an unlikely sex symbol in the early days, but once he had established his distinctive mixture of gaucheness and idealism, his fumbling good humour and lovely smile he quickly became a big box-office draw. This distinctive mixture was most notable in the 1938 screen version of Kaufman and Hart's *You Can't Take It With You*, in which he played the boss's son who falls in love with the only sane member of a loopy household. Like Cooper, his image, in part an extension of his own considerable personality, had a ring of truth which made him liked by men as much as women.

A Pennsylvanian by birth, Stewart came to Hollywood via the New York stage, and was given his first big break as the sailor in the musical *Born to Dance*, 1936, opposite Eleanor Powell. In the next few years he starred successfully with a variety of leading ladies including Claudette Colbert in *It's a Wonderful World*, Jean Arthur in *Mr Smith Goes to Washington*, and Marlene Dietrich in *Destry Rides Again*. According to producer Joe Pasternak, Dietrich 'took one look at him and wanted him at once'. Then, in 1940, he was cast opposite Katharine Hepburn in *The Philadelphia Story*, and won an Oscar, beating Cary Grant.

Without in any way being a personality star, Stewart's private life contributed considerably to his popularity — one of the first screen actors to volunteer for the Second World War, he rose from a $21-a-week private to a colonel

ABOVE: *Mr Smith Goes to Washington*, 1939, with Astrid Allwyn
RIGHT: *The Philadelphia Story*, 1940, with Katharine Hepburn

and won numerous top military honours, including the Distinguished Service Medal. No demon lover in his private life, he remained a stolid bachelor until, in his early forties, he met his wife, Gloria, through Gary Cooper.

Some of Stewart's strongest postwar performances were given in Westerns. His image, like that of Cooper, communicated the sense of honesty and patriotism required of the Western hero: he was powerful hunting down his own brother in *Winchester 73* and moving as the husband of an Indian girl (Debra Paget) in *Broken Arrow*, both made in 1950, but engagingly naive in *The Man Who Shot Liberty Valance*, 1962. In a quite different vein, his humour saved *The Glenn Miller Story*, 1954, from drowning in its own sentimentality. One of his most appealingly funny performances was in *Harvey*, 1950, as Elwood P. Dowd, a friendly soak who has regressed to childhood by postulating a giant rabbit as his invisible playmate. Stewart's endearing charm was also used intriguingly by Hitchcock, who cast him well against type as the voyeur in *Rear Window*, 1954.

ABOVE: portrait, c. 1938
LEFT: *It's a Wonderful Life*, 1947, with Donna Reed

HEDY LAMARR

For a brief while Hedy Lamarr was pro-claimed as the successor to Garbo. Billed by MGM's Louis B. Mayer as 'the most beautiful woman in films', Lamarr was given the full benefit of the MGM publicity machine just as Garbo herself was proving awkward to handle and faltering at the box office. Lamarr certainly projected a distinct, exotic glamour that passed off as vaguely 'European'. But she lacked a distinct charisma or personality to match her beauty. When Mayer realized that this 'next Garbo' was fool's gold, he began to lose interest, particularly since she too was proving difficult to please: she turned down the leads in *Casablanca, Gaslight* and *Saratoga Trunk*, and left the field clear for Ingrid Bergman.

Lamarr had been discovered in Berlin by Max Reinhardt, so the story goes, and achieved notoriety in a Czech film, *Extase*, of 1933. The young Hedwig Kiesler (her real name) was glimpsed running naked through a sylvan glade. A buzz of excitement greeted this artistic performance, which rose to a salacious frenzy when the film was shown in the USA. With prudish reservations Mayer signed this new star, but nervously leased her out to another producer, Walter Wanger. Everything augured well with her first leading role in *Algiers*, 1938, as a be-witching temptress who lures Charles Boyer out of the casbah. But despite the sterling efforts of such slogans as 'You too will be "Hedy" with delight and your verdict will be "Lamarrvel-lous"', her follow-ups generally failed to sparkle.

She was given every inducement: Spencer Tracy for *I Take This Woman*, 1939, Clark Gable for *Boom Town* and *Comrade X*, both 1940, not to mention other leading men like James Stewart, Robert Taylor, Walter Pidgeon and William Powell. *Ziegfeld Girl*, 1941, in which she co-starred with Judy Garland and Lana Turner, remains one of her most entertaining efforts.

RIGHT: studio portrait, 1939.
Photographer Laszlo Willinger

She achieved her finest hour — and her biggest box office hit — in DeMille's gaudy Biblical epic *Samson and Delilah*, 1949, opposite Victor Mature, whose own caricatured good looks and acting prowess were wholly in her own class. Lamarr portrayed Delilah with a healthy disregard for any attempt at realism. Her determination and panache helped make it a box office hit, and amid the ruins of its Technicolor temple, it could be said that she had found her true level at last.

RIGHT: publicity portrait for *Lady of the Tropics*, 1939.
      Photographer Laszlo Willinger
BELOW: publicity portrait for *Lady of the Tropics*, 1939, with Robert Taylor.
      Photographer Clarence Sinclair Bull

CARY GRANT

ABOVE: *Blonde Venus*, 1932, with
Marlene Dietrich
OPPOSITE: studio portrait, 1940.
Photographer Clarence Sinclair Bull

The most universally appealing romantic male lead of his time, Grant himself put his finger on the secret of his attraction: 'I play myself', he once said, 'to perfection.' He sustained an extraordinary high level of performance over a career that stretched from the thirties to the sixties and although he never won an Academy Award as Best Actor, perhaps because of the deceptive ease of his performances, he undoubtedly has a claim to being one of Hollywood's greatest actors. His debonair, carefree charm, natural acting gifts and awesome sense of timing made him a master of thirties light and screwball comedy, outstandingly under the direction of Howard Hawks. Through such films his image became the essence of cultivated urban sophistication, that of the smooth and desirable American male with the right manners and the right physique, a man who would always step competently over the trip-wires of fate on his way to painlessly achieved moral growth. In the forties, however, Hitchcock took Grant's persona of the desirable bachelor as a device to obvert the less appealing qualities implied underneath. In *Suspicion* Grant was cast as a dubious playboy, frightening new wife Joan Fontaine, and in *Notorious*, as a cold, emotionally blocked figure, who practically destroys Ingrid Bergman before saving her through the ultimate recognition and acknowledgement of his own feelings.

Grant did not have a very happy childhood; his mother had a breakdown when he was nine years old and he disliked school, preferring to knock around as a general dogsbody at the Hippodrome Theatre. He ran away from home to join a travelling vaudeville show at the age of thirteen and although he was brought back, he got his father's permission to rejoin when he came of age a year later; it was after a trip to New York, and then a countrywide tour of the United States with the troupe two years later, that he became enthused with the place and decided to settle there.

By 1923, Grant was playing in musical comedies on Broadway under his christened name Archibald Leach, and eight years later, undeterred by his failure to wow talent scouts – who had told him that he was bow-legged and that his neck was too thick – he set off for the West Coast. Having landed a $400-a-week contract, he changed his name to Cary Grant (taking the christian name from one of his Broadway plays and the surname from a studio list of suitable names) and made his debut the next year, in 1932, in *This Is The Night*. He rapidly built up a solid reputation as a leading man, notably in *Blonde Venus* with Marlene Dietrich, *Suzy* with Jean Harlow, *The Awful Truth* with Irene Dunne and two films – *She Done Him Wrong* and *I'm No Angel* – with Mae West, to whom he later attributed his own mastery of comedy, saying that he learned everything from her.

In 1935 he made his first film with Katharine Hepburn, *Sylvia Scarlett*. There was a tremendous chemistry between his dry elegance and her faintly zany astringency, and later in the thirties they co-starred in the classic Howard Hawks comedy, *Bringing Up Baby*. Still working with Hawks, Grant successfully adapted to the adventure genre in *Only Angels Have*

ABOVE: *Holiday*, 1938, with Katharine Hepburn
RIGHT: *Arsenic and Old Lace*, 1944, with Priscilla Lane

Wings, and was also marvellous with Rosalind Russell in the role-reversal *His Girl Friday*, 1940, a remake of *The Front Page*. Paired again by George Cukor with Katharine Hepburn in the comedy of the idle rich, *The Philadelphia Story*, 1940, Grant played the part of her disrespectful ex-husband perfectly; it was a smash hit, and one of the roles for which Grant is remembered by a very wide audience.

The Hawks movies give a hint of the less pleasant aspects of Grant. Although it is usually light-hearted, the ambiguity is there: male chauvinism in *Only Angels Have Wings*, teasing malice in *His Girl Friday*, emotional stagnation in *Bringing Up Baby*. In the latter Hawks uses Grant as a desiccated academic, his dry disaffection reflected in the skeleton of the brontosaurus he is reconstructing for a museum, brought to life only by Hepburn. The suggestion is that Grant's irresistible charm masks qualities of immaturity, self-centredness, misogyny and a certain parsimony of the human spirit. By looking good, he makes others look small — and enjoys doing so.

Not long afterwards, Grant began his fruitful partnership with Alfred Hitchcock, who directed him in *Suspicion*, 1941, opposite Joan Fontaine, and *Notorious*, 1946, opposite Ingrid Bergman. Grant's other two films for Hitchcock, *To Catch a Thief* with Grace Kelly and *North by Northwest* with Eva Marie Saint, both made in the fifties, were immensely successful. Hitchcock once said that there was a great problem with *Suspicion*, because audiences could never believe in Grant as a killer; but through Grant's masterly performances in this and his later work for Hitchcock we can well see the symbiotic relationship between the smooth, competent façade and the cold, unpleasant character beneath. In *North by Northwest*, for

ABOVE: *Suspicion*, 1941, with Joan Fontaine
LEFT: *Only Angels Have Wings*, 1939, with Rita Hayworth

instance, Hitchcock takes that image – the slick, successful charmer who relies on his highly prized appeal to see him through – and by robbing him of his precious identity reduces him to total impotence, from which he can only escape by showing humility and need. It goes without saying that Grant could only evince these ambiguities by being a very great actor with complete technical command.

As Grant aged, he became even more attractive and charismatic, turning the romantic myth of his image – an almost unattainable standard of

RIGHT: studio portrait, 1940.
    Photographer Clarence Sinclair Bull
BELOW: *The Philadelphia Story*, 1940, with
    Katharine Hepburn

masculinity — into fact. This was an important element in the credibility and staying power of his persona with the more honest audiences of the early sixties, when he made the comedy thriller *Charade*, 1963, with Audrey Hepburn. He retired from making movies in the mid-sixties, playing an older man acting cupid to Samantha Eggar and Jim Hutton in his swansong, *Walk Don't Run*, 1966.

His first three marriages, to Virginia Cherrill, Barbara Hutton, the Woolworth heiress, and Betsy Drake, all ended fairly quickly in divorce (he has indicated that his broken adult relationships had their roots in the early loss of his mother) but he had a daughter, Jennifer, at the age of sixty-two by his fourth wife, actress Dyan Cannon.

ABOVE: publicity portrait for *Indiscreet*, 1958
LEFT: *The Pride and the Passion*, 1957, with Sophia Loren

FREDRIC MARCH

A subtle, expressive American, March was one of Hollywood's and Broadway's most distinguished performers, winning two Oscars – for *Dr Jekyll and Mr Hyde* in 1932, and *The Best Years of Our Lives*, 1946 – and making good films in a remarkable variety of genres over his forty-year career. During the thirties he played romantic lead opposite lots of glamorous ladies, notably Garbo in *Anna Karenina*, 1935, although he also worked on Broadway, often with his wife, Florence Eldridge. In much of his work he was essentially a reliable and durable support vehicle for his leading lady. His voice and looks were well suited to comedy, and he gave a notable performance in Ernst Lubitsch's *Design for Living*.

March had planned a career in banking, but decided while recovering from an attack of appendicitis in his early twenties that acting would be more fun. His film career took off after he recreated the role of John Barrymore, the Great Profile, in the screen version of *The Royal Family of Broadway* and he played the first of the fading film stars in *A Star Is Born*, 1937, leading the way for James Mason and Kris Kristofferson in later remakes. He demonstrated his versatility by taking on Carole Lombard in the screwball comedy *Nothing Sacred* in the same year. When he got too old to be a romantic hero he took on character roles with great distinction.

ABOVE: publicity portrait for
    The Night Angel, 1931
LEFT: *Anna Karenina*, 1935, with Greta Garbo

OPPOSITE: publicity portrait for *Letty Lynton*,
    1932.
    Photographer George Hurrell

Joan Crawford survived everything. She was a star for fifty years, and she seemed able to rise above all the irrelevancies of hack plots, her ham acting and the bad reviews. It was more important to her that audiences loved her — and they did so in their thousands throughout the many phases in Crawford's career, involving change after change to her looks and hairstyle. She had been a silent Jazz Baby in the twenties, a Working-Class Girl Making Good in the early thirties, MGM Glamour Queen in the late thirties, and Washed-Up Star by the early forties. Yet, with the Oscar-winning success of *Mildred Pierce*,

RIGHT: *The Taxi Dancer*, 1927, with Owen Moore
BELOW: publicity portrait for *Grand Hotel*, 1932.
Photographer George Hurrell

1945, the quintessential Crawford movie, she bounced back from the ropes to start afresh in the post-war era. She became a late-forties Career Woman, a camp Bitch Goddess of the fifties, and, after *Whatever Happened to Baby Jane?*, 1962, metamorphosed into the Monstrous Gorgon, her last disguise and the one for which she is ironically best remembered. 'Poor Joan', as one of her fan-magazine headlines might have put it. For somewhere between the bright-eyed flapper girl of *Our Dancing Daughters*, 1928, and the grotesque portrait of her as a real-life Cruella De Ville in *Mommie Dearest*, 1981, is the story of

LEFT: studio portrait, c. 1932.
Photographer George Hurrell
BELOW: *Strange Cargo*, 1940, with Clark Gable

a twentieth-century American woman devoured by the single thing she loved most – stardom.

Crawford's ruthless ambition was evident from the beginning. She was born as Lucille Fay Le Sueur in San Antonio, Texas, and had worked as a Kansas City shopgirl and waitress, a Chicago dancer and a Detroit chorus girl before she arrived in Hollywood aged twenty-one, doubling for Norma Shearer. Her name was changed, in Crawford's case via a nationwide publicity contest, and after hoofing it through several good-time epics, *Our Dancing Daughters* put that new name in lights. Through *Paid*, 1930, a debut with Clark Gable in *Possessed*, 1931, and alongside Garbo as a typist-on-the-make in *Grand Hotel*, 1932, Crawford found a niche as everyone's favourite working girl. Despite a failure in the dramatic role of Sadie Thompson in *Rain*, 1932, she went on to grab better roles for herself in *Dancing Lady*, 1933, opposite Gable, and in a series of star vehicles from *Today We Live*, 1933, to *The Last of Mrs Cheyney*, 1937.

Throughout the thirties Crawford's features peered out regularly from the covers of the fan magazines and women's weeklies, and in 1938, when she was voted 'box office poison' by US exhibitors, MGM could counter-attack by saying that Crawford had received a phenomenal total of 900,000 fan letters. (Some contemporary Hollywood wits said they could imagine Crawford counting every one.) If familiarity had bred contempt by then, with Frank Borzage's *Mannequin*, 1937, and especially with Cukor's *The Women*, 1939, Crawford proved that there were directors in Hollywood who could profitably exploit her tough glamour, brittle passions and vivid sense of melodrama. But after two more years MGM let her go free-lance. She signed up with Warners,

ABOVE: studio portrait, c. 1935.
Photographer George Hurrell
RIGHT: *Chained*, 1934, with Clark Gable

but had to plead with them for the lead in the *film noir* melodrama *Mildred Pierce*. As a housewife sacrificing herself for her spiteful and thankless daughter, Crawford played the part of her life with a wide-eyed zeal that was awesome. Her face was harder, fiercer than before, with a mouth painted like a clown's; her prize of an Oscar must have seemed sweet revenge.

Humoresque, 1946, *Flamingo Road*, 1949, and *This Woman is Dangerous*, 1952, all proved that she was in her prime, her face portraying renewed passion and determination with the fixed intensity of an eastern goddess. Even in the highlights of her fifties career, such as the baroque operatic Western, *Johnny Guitar*, 1954, Crawford seemed to inhabit a different

plane to her co-stars, who could only cower in her presence. It was as if she had been taken over by a demon power, and Robert Aldrich used that not-so-latent quality of madness to great effect in the riveting *Whatever Happened to Baby Jane?* With less sure direction, that same quality also produced cheap trash like *Berserk*, 1967, and *Trog*, 1970, two films in which Crawford's image came very close indeed to the sinister harridan portrayed in *Mommie Dearest*, her daughter's vengeful biography of her.

F. Scott Fitzgerald once wrote of her, 'She can't change her emotions in the middle of a scene without going through a sort of Jekyll and Hyde contortion of the face.' But she did show that cinema acting is not so much a

question of dramatic subtlety as one of sheer presence and charisma – even if, at times, one cannot quite be sure that she is actually acting at all.

ABOVE: *Above Suspicion*, 1943, with Fred MacMurray

ROBERT TAYLOR

Taylor was a perfectly proportioned piece of beefcake whose flawless, glowing handsomeness personified male strength. He had thousands of besotted female fans and became a huge box-office draw; when he sailed to England to make *A Yank At Oxford* with Vivien Leigh in 1938, thousands of women waited for him on the quay at Southampton — and a handful were unearthed from under his bed. His acting ability was decidedly modest, but he made a tremendous leading man for some of Hollywood's strongest ladies in the thirties and forties. Off-screen, however, he was a peaceful man who avoided embroilment in

OPPOSITE: studio portrait, 1936.
Photographer Ted Allan
LEFT: *Personal Property*, 1938, with Jean Harlow
BELOW: *The Gorgeous Hussy*, 1936, with
Joan Crawford

shattering personal events: a docile, grateful and uncomplaining exployee, he stayed with MGM for twenty-six years. He was married twice, to Barbara Stanwyck and Ursula Thiess.

It is tempting to suggest that Taylor's popularity with strong leading ladies was due mainly to the fact that he just stood around looking beautiful and let them get on with the acting. He throbbed at Garbo in *Camille* and gazed mooningly at Jean Harlow in *Personal Property*, but there was something innocuous and docile about him. Unlike Errol Flynn, his gorgeous features were not animated by the suggestion that he was capable of being a very bad boy indeed. Taylor summed up his early career himself: 'I was awful, the world's worst actor. But I had a couple of good things going for me – I was a good-looking kid and had a good voice. So I got the breaks.'

Born Spangler Arlington Brough, he studied music at college, where he was spotted by an MGM talent scout playing the lead in the dramatic society's production of 'Journey's End'. He took up MGM's offer of a $35-a-week contract, became Robert Taylor, and launched into his heyday with the classic weepie, *Magnificent Obsession*, 1935, playing a drunken playboy who reforms and becomes selflessly devoted to Irene Dunne. He swept audiences off their feet and within a year had played opposite some of the best leading ladies: Janet Gaynor in *Small Town Girl*, Loretta Young in *Private Number*, Barbara Stanwyck in *His Brother's Wife*, Joan Crawford in *The Gorgeous Hussy* and Greta Garbo in *Camille*. Over the next few years his image became tougher. He played a prize-fighter opposite Maureen O'Sullivan in *The Crowd Roars*, 1938, and a once-rich boy forced to work, and fight, for his living in *Stand Up and Fight*, 1939. By then he had been paired with Vivien Leigh

OPPOSITE: studio portrait, 1936.
Photographer Frank Grimes
RIGHT: *Camille*, 1937, with Greta Garbo

for the first time in *A Yank At Oxford* and two years later they came together again for his own favourite movie, the weepie *Waterloo Bridge* in which she is a ballerina forced to take to the streets and he is a dashing officer who is her unsuspecting lover. As he himself commented, 'I was never a good actor, I guess, but they sure put me in some good movies'.

Like many of his contemporaries, Taylor did not find it easy to pick up his career after the war, during which he had spent two years as a flying instructor and narrated *The Fighting Lady*, an award-winning documentary about a warship. But MGM remembered his loyalty and managed to find him roles in some classy films: *Quo Vadis*, 1951, in which he played a Roman centurion in love with a Christian, Deborah Kerr, sustained his reputation, and he followed up with more costume movies, most memorably *Ivanhoe* – made in 1952, the same year he and Barbara Stanwyck were divorced – and *The Knights of the Round Table*, 1954, in which he played Lancelot. He also made some reasonable Westerns. In 1959, he finally broke with MGM to go freelance, played for several years in the television series, 'The Detectives', and made a handful of not very memorable films before he died in 1969.

ABOVE: *Lucky Night*, 1939, with Myrna Loy
RIGHT: *Johnny Eager*, 1942, with Lana Turner

ABOVE: publicity portrait for *Shanghai Express*, 1932.
Photographer Don English

Dietrich herself would have it that the world's first glimpse of her was on her entrance in *Der blaue Engel/The Blue Angel*, 1930. As the teasing vamp Lola Lola she perched tantalizingly on stage, held out her long stocking-clad legs for approval, tilted her mannish top hat rakishly to one side, and delivered a rendition of 'Falling in Love Again' with such languorous eroticism that, in James Agate's memorable phrase, she seemed to make 'reason totter on her throne'. As she enslaved the hapless schoolteacher Emil Jannings to her every whim, she created a seductively androgynous fantasy female that was the great achievement of herself and director Josef von

Sternberg, during the six films they made together for Paramount over the following years.

It mattered little that this 'new Garbo' was already in her late twenties and the mother of a five-year-old daughter, nor that she had been appearing in movies since 1923. For the Dietrich myth was, from the very moment that Sternberg saw her performing on stage, a monument to elaborate artifice and teasing ambiguity. In *Morocco*, 1930, *Dishonored*, 1931, *Shanghai Express*, 1932, *Blonde Venus*, 1932, *The Scarlet Empress*, 1934, and *The Devil is a Woman*, 1935, she, Sternberg and cinematographers Lee Garmes and

Bert Glennon perfected a Dietrich who was an elusive and exotic figment of the imagination. Swathed in veils and feathers, criss-crossed in patterns of light, she was as beguiling and inaccessible as a goddess. Compared with Garbo's realism, Dietrich was intended as a figure of illusion, beyond belief and as magical as the flickering image of cinema itself. She rightfully belonged in the Paramount-style *demi-monde* of Morocco or Shanghai, where her siren qualities could lure in every bar-room Ulysses like Gary Cooper or Clive Brook who should stumble unsuspectingly upon her.

RIGHT: studio portrait, 1930.
 Photographer Eugene Robert Richee
BELOW: *The Garden of Allah*, 1936, with
 Charles Boyer

Dietrich and Sternberg experimented as she grew in popularity, and adorned her body in an increasingly fetishistic manner. Her masculine appearance in top hat and tails or men's suits lent an intriguing sexual ambiguity to her persona, and set a fashion in the early thirties that evoked a vague reminder of Weimar decadence and perversity. She was merely a cabaret singer for *Morocco*, but became a Mata Hari-type spy clad in black leather for *Dishonored*; and as the infamous Shanghai Lily in *Shanghai Express* she draped herself in feather boas and veils. *The Scarlet Empress*

LEFT: publicity portrait for *Shanghai Express*, 1932.
Photographer Don English
BELOW: *Blonde Venus*, 1932, with Cary Grant

allowed her to indulge in the extravagantly regal costumes of Catherine the Great, and in *Blonde Venus* and *The Devil is a Woman* she became increasingly immobile under a bewildering array of wigs, slit skirts, shimmering dresses and even a gorilla suit. These disguises knowingly aroused desires which her character proceeded to dismiss with contempt. For her persona was built around the supremely romantic notion that love is impossible. She lived in a never-changing world of obsession and devotion – a long way indeed from the Hollywood ideal of cosy married bliss.

Disappointing box office returns for *The Devil is a Woman* reduced Paramount's confidence in their actor–director partnership, and it was to be Dietrich's last film with Von Sternberg. Her career now slid dramatically. Even directors like Frank Borzage (*Desire*, 1936) or Ernst Lubitsch (*Angel*, 1937) could not recapture her magic. She dropped to 126th place in the box office polls, and Paramount bought out her contract. They had tried to use her as an actress, but her technique had been misunderstood. She was actually the charismatic central figure of an aesthetic, and could no more adapt to a different style than a statue can alter its pose.

Dietrich did return in a comic role in *Destry Rides Again*, 1939, was admired by both John Wayne and Randolph Scott in *Spoilers*, 1942, and recovered some of her old exoticism when she was painted gold for *Kismet*, 1944. During the war she entertained US troops and made anti-Nazi propaganda broadcasts in her native German, but as an actress she remained under-used until 1948, when Billy Wilder's *A Foreign Affair* set her in the ruins of Berlin after the war. By then she had adopted a new career as a *chanteuse*, and her legendary nightclub

LEFT: publicity photograph for *Shanghai Express*, 1932, with and by photographer Don English

act resurrected again and again the memory of the thirties Dietrich – even if she herself tetchily dismissed those early movies of hers. She has returned to films only infrequently, most tellingly in Orson Welles' *Touch of Evil*, 1958, in which she somehow played the madame of a Mexican saloon with effortless conviction. *Judgment at Nuremberg*, 1961, could be justified, but *Schöner Gigolo – Armer Gigolo/Just a Gigolo*, 1978, could not: it was a disappointing full stop to a movie career that had effectively halted more than forty years ago.

RIGHT: portrait, 1935.
    Photographer Eugene Robert Richee
BELOW: *Destry Rides Again*, 1939, with
    James Stewart

CLARK GABLE

In *Broadway Melody of 1938*, Judy Garland gazes at a photograph and sings 'Dear Mr Gable, you made me love you', a sentence which mirrored the sentiments of thousands of fans of the time. Gable's stupendous charisma made him King of Hollywood, carried him through the thirty years of changing fashion in masculinity, and brought him a series of classic leading roles, stretching from *Red Dust* in 1932 to *The Misfits*, his last film in 1961. Gable was essentially a man of the people: a plain-spoken, tough boy from small-town America who never put on unnatural airs or graces, and had little time for women who did; look at the way he slapped rich bitch Norma Shearer around in *A Free Soul*.

Gable was particularly proud of one of his acting techniques — while his female co-stars melted under his lusty, lingering gazes, he was actually thinking of a piece of prime, juicy steak. The technique certainly worked. Cynical, self-assured and extremely sexy, his host of leading ladies reads like a roll-call of all-time greats: Mary Astor, Jean Harlow, Greta Garbo, Joan Crawford, Vivien Leigh, Carole Lombard, Hedy Lamarr and Marilyn Monroe. While he could be passionate and protective, he never swooned over his women, instead cheerfully treating them as equals and expecting them to reciprocate with honesty and integrity — or face the consequences. In one of his first big successes, *It Happened One Night*, 1934, his thumb-on-the-nose reporter typically fell in with a society miss (Claudette Colbert), refused to treat her like a lady and won her over, almost literally at the final curtain, when the blanket that primly divided their room came tumbling down. His direct earthiness and offer of a certain kind of sexual democracy was universally appealing. He also had a huge

OPPOSITE: studio portrait, 1937.
Photographer Laszlo Willinger
ABOVE: *Dancing Lady*, 1933, with Joan Crawford
LEFT: *No Man of Her Own*, 1932, with Carole Lombard

87

influence upon men, as was shown by the drop in profits of the American underwear industry when he took off his shirt in *It Happened One Night* to reveal only his bare, extremely manly chest beneath.

Gable retained his charisma and personality off the screen and his lack of pretension and amusement at his own physical flaws – he used to say that he had ears like a pair of garage doors and let it be known that his teeth were not all his own – made him all the more attractive. Married twice before he became a star, first to Josephine Dillon, a one-time actress thirteen

RIGHT: Publicity portrait for *Boom Town*, 1940, with Hedy Lamarr
BELOW: *Honky Tonk*, 1941, with Lana Turner

years his senior who gave him coaching and helped him up the movie ladder, and then to Ria Langham, another older woman, he diverted himself over the next decade with numerous fleeting affairs and one-night stands with a maelstrom of females both celebrated and obscure. One of his entanglements was with Joan Crawford, who later remarked, 'He had balls', but the tough, beautiful hoyden Carole Lombard, whom he married in 1939, was probably his one great love. They had no chance to become disenchanted: early in 1942,

LEFT: *After Office Hours*, 1935, with
Constance Bennett
BELOW: *Strange Cargo*, 1940, with
Joan Crawford

at the age of thirty-four she was killed in a plane crash. He went looking for her in the wreckage, utterly traumatized by her death.

By that time, Gable had reached the peak of his career. He had drifted through various jobs — salesman, lumberjack, reporter and truck driver — and survived rejection from both Warner Brothers and MGM (after John Barrymore had suggested they screen-test him) before becoming a major star in the early thirties. He turned in some crackling love scenes with Jean Harlow in *Red Dust*, 1932, won an Academy Award for his performance in the Frank Capra comedy, *It Happened One Night*, and gave a lovely performance opposite Jeanette MacDonald in *San Francisco*. His ultimate movie was still to come. Margaret Mitchell, the author of *Gone With The Wind*, is reputed to have had Gable's screen persona in mind when she created the character of 'Frankly, my dear, I don't give a damn' Rhett Butler; certainly, fiction and flesh are hard to distinguish and Gable's portrayal is a crucial factor in the success of Selznick's film. Unchivalrous, baldly lustful, knowing and cocking a snook at all social and emotional pretension, the Butler/Gable character overshadowed many modern screen heroes.

Shortly after Lombard's death — her last cable to him read, 'Pappy, you'd better join this man's army' — Gable finished his shooting commitments on *Somewhere I'll Find You* and enlisted as a private in the air force, remaining there for the rest of the war. He teamed up with Greer Garson, whom he loathed, for his return to the screen in *Adventure*, 1945, but it was a failure and after that he made few memorable films. His popularity remained as strong as ever, but, by now middle-aged, he was uneasy in the role of romantic male lead that producers persisted in assigning to him. His most

ABOVE: *Red Dust*, 1932, with Jean Harlow
RIGHT: *Red Dust*, with Mary Astor

successful post-war film was, perhaps, *Mogambo*, 1953, John Ford's remake of *Red Dust*, playing opposite Ava Gardner and Grace Kelly. Meanwhile, his private life continued choppily. He married twice more, first to Sylvia, Lady Ashley and then to Kay Spreckels, who looked like Carole Lombard and produced Gable's only child, a son, after his death.

Gable's last performance, tough, earthily sexy and never more poignant, as the aging cowboy lover of Marilyn Monroe in *The Misfits*, 1961, was hailed by the critics as the outstanding performance of his career. Full of ironies about aging, love and male vitality, it can be seen as Gable reviewing his own masculinity. He died in November 1960, a few weeks after shooting finished.

ABOVE: *The Misfits*, 1961
LEFT: *Mogambo*, 1953, with Grace Kelly

GINGER ROGERS

Astaire and Rogers in motion were a blissful union. She was bubbly, brash, colourful, real-life; he was cool, dapper, black and white, abstract. As cheek to cheek they glide over those gleaming floors, love and romance seem to come to life on the screen, eclipsing the real world and making it seem tawdry and irrelevant. In ten classic movies with Astaire, reaching its acme with *Swing Time*, 1936, Rogers sparkles like a bright gem, adding visible warmth and humanity to the austere brilliance of Astaire.

The vaudeville circuit was the first stop on Rogers' rise to stardom, and from there she got work for various film studios. There was a quality of toughness about Rogers, even in her films with Astaire, that served her well in this period, in her roles as a gum-chewing, wisecracking broad: she was one of the girls sharing a world-weary giggle in Warner's *42nd Street*, 1933, and an eager cynic in a go-getting world in *Gold Diggers of 1933*. Her next major film was at RKO, and with Astaire; but in 1939 after *The Story of Vernon and Irene Castle*, Rogers went her own way. She quickly proved her professionalism in *Kitty Foyle*, 1940, for which she won the Best Actress Oscar: as a salesgirl who lands a rich man, but who begins to hanker after one of her own kind, the role is a good example of Rogers' appeal to young girls of her own class. Rogers was best in comedy, as when she breezily holds a court to ransom with her sob story and hitched-up skirt as *Roxie Hart*, 1942. Her film career continued throughout the fifties, and she had great success both on Broadway and the London stage in the sixties. But she never found as complementary a leading man as Astaire. Apart, they each graduated to their respective worlds; but together, they defined romance.

RIGHT: publicity portrait for *Once Upon a Honeymoon*, 1942, with Cary Grant. Photographer John Miehle

FRED ASTAIRE

Genial and elegant but ultimately elusive as a screen persona, Astaire's bewitching power was in his movement. He was once described as the 'vertical expression of horizontal desire', and his legs were insured for $300,000. He headed for Hollywood after his elder sister, Adele, had retired from their dazzlingly successful dance partnership on Broadway and fortunately survived his first Hollywood screen test, which offered the discouraging verdict, 'Can't act. Slightly bald. Can dance a little'.

It was at RKO that he formed his legendary partnership with Ginger Rogers. No one has ever danced like them, before or since. Their extraordinary chemistry was explosive in movies like *The Gay Divorcee*, 1934, *Top Hat*, 1935, *Roberta*, 1935, and *Swing Time*, 1936. She could not match his skill but brought colour and sensuality to his airy grace, or as Katharine Hepburn put it, 'He gave her class, she gave him sex'.

When Ginger Rogers virtually gave up dancing in the late thirties, Astaire became debonair playboy consort to a series of leading ladies like Eleanor Powell, Rita Hayworth, Judy Garland, Cyd Charisse and Audrey Hepburn. There is a school of thought that after Rogers he was zero, but he had great sequences with Charisse in *The Band Wagon*, and was brilliant, as was Hepburn, in *Funny Face*. He remained as commanding and dominant as ever and when he was pitted against his great rival, Gene Kelly, in *Ziegfeld Follies*, 1946, he won on points.

Astaire went on to play convincing straight dramatic roles in later life such as *On The Beach*, 1959, and *The Towering Inferno*, 1974. In 1949 he received his special Academy Award for 'unique artistry and his contributions to the technique of motion pictures' — a long-winded way of saying he was magic.

RIGHT: publicity portrait for *Broadway Melody of 1940*
OVER: Cary Grant and Ingrid Bergman, publicity portrait for *Notorious*, 1946. Photographer Ernest A. Bachrach

THE WAR YEARS

ERROL FLYNN

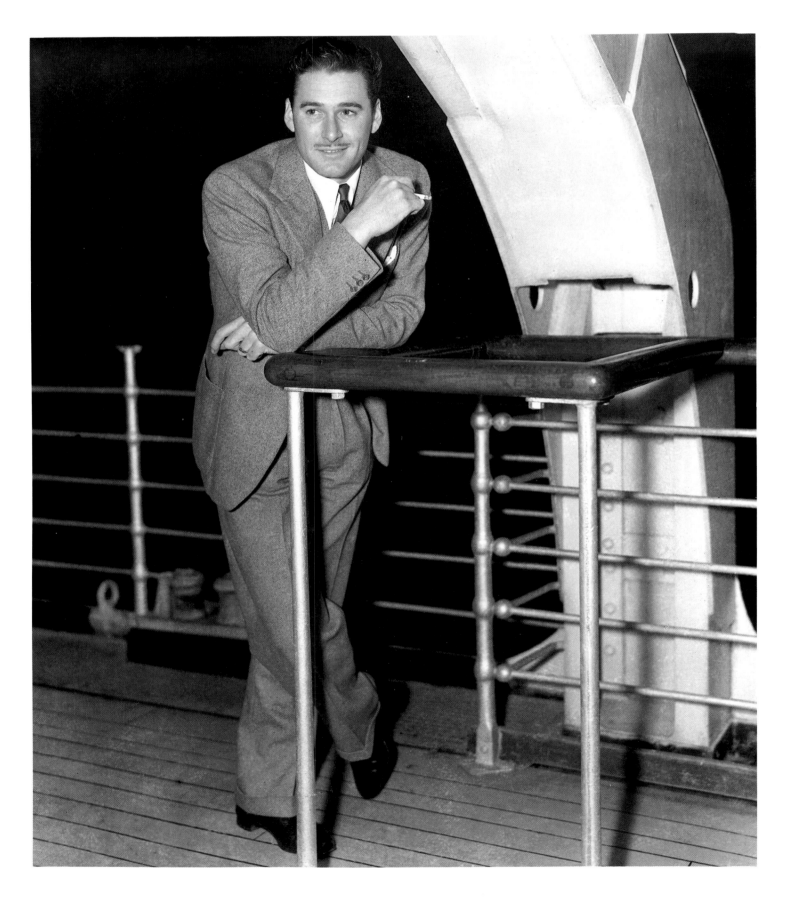

Errol Flynn was one of the most handsome and romantic leading men to come out of Hollywood. A gallant, with a graceful animal presence, his virile exploits made him the embodiment of male dreams and the object of female fantasies. His private life, however, was unruly and tragic. He lived for years on the edge of disaster and eventually fell from grace and became an object of anger and ridicule.

He came to Hollywood from the English stage, bouncing to stardom in the mid-thirties with another new face, Olivia de Havilland, in *Captain Blood*, 1935. Their magnificent chemistry made *The Charge of the Light Brigade*, 1936, *The Adventures of Robin Hood*, 1938, and *They Died With*

OPPOSITE: portrait, c. 1939
LEFT: *The Adventures of Robin Hood*, 1938, with Olivia De Havilland
BELOW: portrait, c. 1935

97

Their Boots On, 1941, enormous box-office successes. Like Doug Fairbanks Sr, his guiding principle as a leading man was never to settle for taking a lady out to dinner when he could be scaling a castle wall to rescue her from the Sheriff of Nottingham. These were Flynn's golden years when he was a giant star and the darling of Hollywood with an adoring public, studio and press. He starred in *The Dawn Patrol* with David Niven, matched Bette Davis in *The Private Lives of Elizabeth and Essex*, 1939, tamed the West in *Dodge City* and swashbuckled in *The Sea Hawk*; always in the role of the brave, manly hero who was not fully dressed without a sword between his teeth or a longbow in his hand.

Flynn's early life was as adventurous as that depicted in any of his films. Born in Tasmania, the son of a marine biologist, he had an unhappy relationship with his mother and took off for Papua New Guinea at the age of seventeen, having been expelled from numerous institutes of learning. There he tried his hand at gold mining, managed a tobacco plantation and worked as a patrol officer, smoking opium and fighting Japanese in China along the way.

Soon afterwards, Flynn married the French actress Lili Damita. Far from a model husband, and with a reputation as a stud, his exploits were laughed off until the end of 1942, when he was charged with having sex with two under-age girls. The court case destroyed him, despite the fact that he was acquitted. He divorced Lili, remarried and fathered two girls, then divorced again and married Patrice Wymore in 1950. In the meantime, though he continued to appear in major films, notably *The Sun Also Rises*, 1957, his popularity had flagged. He drank a great deal, had a last fling with a teenage girlfriend, and died in 1959.

ABOVE: *Dodge City*, 1939, with Olivia De Havilland
RIGHT: *Against All Flags*, 1946, with Maureen O'Hara

Alan Ladd could never understand his own popularity; only 5ft 6in tall, he had to stand on boxes to meet other actors in the eye, and he once described his build as that of an undernourished featherweight. But he was also extremely handsome with an air of downbeat, withdrawn violence and a look of psychological suffering that made him equally attractive as a taciturn, vulnerable good or bad guy. Ladd became a star overnight after his portrayal of the fair, trench-coated killer in *This Gun for Hire* in 1942, and stayed on top for twenty years despite a relative dearth of good films. His most memorable part was in the epic Western *Shane*, which used Ladd's screen image to suggest the covert ruthlessness that made the character believable.

The son of an accountant who died when he was three, Ladd had grown up in California during the Depression, taken various odd jobs, and worked as an extra and a technician before honing his distinctive voice on radio and marrying his agent, Sue Carol. The film parts began to come in and after the success of his casting opposite Veronica Lake in *This Gun for Hire*, they were teamed up again for *The Glass Key*, 1942, and *The Blue Dahlia*, 1946, both good little-guy thrillers. Well after the peak of his career came *Shane* in 1953, but it was an epic performance, with Ladd as the gunfighter trying to give up his trade, but forced to kill in order to save the lives of others. Ladd later refused the offer of the James Dean role in *Giant*, and towards the end of the fifties he lost his looks, drank heavily and made largely unremembered films, dying at the age of fifty-one from an overdose of sedatives mixed with alcohol.

RIGHT: publicity portrait for *This Gun for Hire*, 1942, with Veronica Lake

BETTE DAVIS

When Bette Davis rebelled against her studio bosses at Warner Bros. in 1937, she could have been acting out a page from one of her own scripts – or at least the kind of script she *wanted* to get. This fierce, twenty-eight-year-old New Englander had fought her way from provincial theatre school into the first rank of Hollywood stars, was already considered an unparalleled movie actress with an Oscar for *Dangerous*, 1935, to prove it, and knew she was worth more than a re-hashed version of 'The Maltese Falcon', even if it was called *Satan Met a*

OPPOSITE: studio portrait, c. 1939.
Photographer George Hurrell
LEFT: studio portrait, c. 1933.
Photographer Elmer Fryer
BELOW: *The Petrified Forest*, 1936, with Leslie Howard

Lady, 1936. So she packed her bags and left for England, intending to end the battles over parts with Warners and make a movie out of contract. Warners slapped an injunction on her. She contested it. A court case followed, and the movie world held its breath. Warners were held to be legally in the right in claiming that her contract ran exclusively for another five years. But Davis was the true victor; after that nobody would push her around again.

That incident from her own life was uncannily typical of her movies. Ever since her debut in *Bad Sister*, 1931, and even as the scheming waitress in RKO's *Of Human Bondage*, 1934, she had made the tough-hearted melodrama her dominion. No matter how bad the script – and it was often really terrible – Davis managed to summon up an overpowering conviction in the material that was always her saving grace. No matter that she tended towards ham as she dished out verbal torture with unashamed relish, she always left an audience convinced of her emotional sincerity. She was for that reason alone the top screen actress of her day.

After her legal battle with Warners, her talent was more justly exploited with a succession of vintage roles, as a Southern belle in *Jezebel*, 1938, suffering a brain tumour and blindness in *Dark Victory*, 1939, madness in *Juarez*, 1939, pining for Errol Flynn in *The Private Lives of Elizabeth and Essex*, 1939, and falling in love with Charles Boyer in *All This and Heaven Too*, 1940. After shooting her lover in *The Letter*, 1940, she went from strength to strength in *The Little Foxes*, 1941, *Now, Voyager*, 1942, and *Mr Skeffington*, 1944.

After this long run of successes, *The Corn is Green*, 1945, started a series of flops. It seemed that Davis had at last

ABOVE: *Jezebel*, 1938, with Henry Fonda
RIGHT: publicity portrait for *The Little Foxes*, 1941.
Photographer Ned Scott

out-stayed her welcome, and in 1949 she was finally released from her Warners contract. If she had vanished then, it could have been said that she thrived best on the welter of hidden emotions of those uncertain war years, and that America in peacetime was unsympathetic to her acid personality. However, no-one reckoned with *All About Eve*, 1950, when Davis took over from Claudette Colbert as the vitriolic Margo Channing. In retrospect, it seems absurd that anyone else but Davis should have been approached to play the spitefully bitchy, but absolutely charming, Margo. The dialogue flew from Davis' mouth like poisoned darts, and she proved, once again, that she was indeed a force to be reckoned with.

Perhaps it was not her fault if Davis' movies after *The Virgin Queen*, 1955, failed to live up to her earlier successes. Some would blame it on her own egotism, others on timidity on the part of the studios. Nevertheless Davis was to pull more surprises out of the hat. *Whatever Happened to Baby Jane?*, 1962, allowed her to exercise freely that talent for Grand Guignol that had never been far beneath her acting style. It was an unexpected success. In both this and its follow-up, *Hush . . . Hush Sweet Charlotte*, 1964, she surprised critics and public by her sincere conviction, a conviction that spilled over into less subtle, more camp offerings like *The Nanny*, 1965, and *The Anniversary*, 1967. In her autobiography *The Lonely Life* published in 1962 Davis declared, 'I'll never make the mistake of saying I'm retired. You do that and you're finished. You just have to make sure you play older and older parts. Hell, I could do a million of those character roles. But I'm stubborn about playing the lead. I'd like to go out with my name above the title.' Movie stars don't come much older than Bette Davis; now well into her

ABOVE: *The Great Lie*, 1941, with George Brent
LEFT: publicity portrait for *The Letter*, 1940.
Photographer George Hurrell

eighties her sinewy body is worn and frail but her powerhouse mind seems as determined as ever. Even in *Death on the Nile*, 1978, she managed to spit some life into the kind of star vehicle she used to drive single-handed in the good old days, when her strength and vitality were at their peak.

RIGHT: publicity portrait for *Now, Voyager*, 1942.
        Photographer Bert Six
BELOW: *All About Eve*, 1950, with Gary Merrill

VIVIEN LEIGH

It is puzzling, to say the least, that an eminent British stage actress should come to scoop two of Hollywood's most prestigious roles: as Scarlett O'Hara in *Gone With the Wind*, 1939, and as Blanche Dubois in *A Streetcar Named Desire*, 1951. They are both quintessentially American characters, both Southern belles, both difficult and complex parts offering formidable obstacles to success. Yet Vivien Leigh made them her own, winning two Oscars in the process. Perhaps, as is often said, people recognized a little bit of Leigh herself in the characters: Scarlett was bold, impetuous, demanding and overreaching; Blanche was faded, neurotic, self-dramatizing and very sad. Both were ultimately unsympathetic and tragically flawed, and in that verdict lies the key to Vivien Leigh's own story.

She rose to prominence in the London theatre in the late thirties, and after playing opposite Laurence Olivier in *Fire Over England* and *21 Days*, both 1937 and both for Alexander Korda, she shone as Ophelia to Olivier's Hamlet in the stage production. Her other British films included a role as Robert Taylor's leading lady in *A Yank at Oxford*, 1938. She first went to Hollywood to join Olivier, by then her lover, and it was fortuitous that preparations for *Gone With the Wind* should be in full swing – but with no-one yet chosen to play opposite Clark Gable. Legend has it that she was introduced to producer David O. Selznick as Scarlett O'Hara, and any indecision was quashed by a superb screen test. To Gable's Rhett Butler she is the perfect match: he is resourceful, exciting and roguish; she is intense, hot-tempered and highly strung. Together they are charming screen lovers, giving performances which somehow manage to rise above the fiery sunsets, cannonfire and cast of thousands.

LEFT: *Fire Over England*, 1937, with Laurence Olivier

She married Olivier in 1940, high on success with both their stars shining brightly; for a short while they were the world's most brilliant couple. But although they were teamed in Korda's American costume drama, *That Hamilton Woman*, 1941, it had been decided, much to her annoyance, that her leading man in *Waterloo Bridge*, 1940, should be Robert Taylor. Her Selznick contract was by now hampering her own wishes, and it was only in the costly *Caesar and Cleopatra*, 1945, that she hit a role which corresponded to her status, if not her talents.

On screen Leigh could project a dazzling array of moods. She was alternately flirtatious and kittenish, then monstrously overbearing and vengeful, switching in the blink of an eye. The change was alarming, sometimes shocking, but always dramatically effective. If it seemed purely the technique of a skilled actress, that assumption was unfortunately undermined as rumours of serious mental illness began to reach the public ear. Although she continued acting, her battle against tuberculosis and her mental condition began to consume her energies, and her career was subsequently erratic. She died in 1967.

At her best, notably in *Gone With the Wind* and *A Streetcar Named Desire*, Leigh was utterly magnetic and quite unlike any of her competitors, with an ability to communicate a depth of feeling at which others could only hint. It is tragic that her instinctive flair for the drama of a character's self-destruction should have been converted, as with other actresses, into gripping material for a true-life showbiz spectacle.

ABOVE: *Gone With the Wind*, 1939, with
　　　Clark Gable
RIGHT: publicity portrait for *Gone With
　　　the Wind*, 1939.
　　　Photographer Laszlo Willinger
OPPOSITE: studio portrait, 1939.
　　　Photographer Eugene Robert Richee

For three decades Barbara Stanwyck was one of Hollywood's most reliable leading ladies, with an enviable range and longevity. She starred opposite a young Clark Gable in the early thirties; and she was still dynamite, literally, in Sam Fuller's phallic Western, *Forty Guns*, 1957. Yet her relatively low status today is a puzzle. She vied with Joan Crawford and Bette Davis as an interpreter of roles for strong women, outshining Crawford's talent for melodrama without resorting to camp, and well able to match Davis quip for quip

LEFT: publicity portrait for *Ball of Fire*, 1941, with Gary Cooper.
Photographer George Hurrell
BELOW: *Double Indemnity*, 1944, with Fred MacMurray and Tom Powers

in her acid-flavoured drawl. Even in terms of temperament she was beyond reproach. But for some reason her image lacks the grandeur of either Davis' or Crawford's. Why?

A glance at three performances which won her Oscar nominations gives some idea. In *Double Indemnity*, 1944, she defines the bewitching *femme fatale* of the rest of the decade in a devastating portrayal of a middle-class Medusa involved in murder. Dressed and bobbed like some blonde voodoo doll, she fixes accomplice Fred MacMurray with a cute smile – but she can turn wicked with the twitch of an eyebrow. Only seven years before Stanwyck had tugged at the heartstrings as a long-suffering mother in *Stella Dallas*, 1937; and in between she was the wisecracking singer Sugarpuss O'Shea who charmed a bumbling professor (Gary Cooper) in the vintage screwball comedy *Ball of Fire*, 1941. In all three Stanwyck avoids that triumph of personality over part that gave her rivals such long-lived distinction. From the fresh-faced Yankee heroine in love with a Chinese warlord in *The Bitter Tea of General Yen*, 1932, to the hard-boiled matriarch opposite Ronald Reagan in *Cattle Queen of Montana*, 1954, Stanwyck could play them all. With her fluid and suggestive looks she could act the tough-hearted thirties gold digger, yet could project an open-eyed enthusiasm as convincingly as a soured spinster's revenge.

Stanwyck's performance in *Double Indemnity* has rarely been bettered; but in the *film noir* cycle of *The Two Mrs Carrolls*, 1946, *Sorry, Wrong Number*, 1948 (which brought another Oscar nomination), and *The File On Thelma Jordan*, 1949, she gave three more performances which would each suffice as the high point of any one actress' career.

ABOVE: studio portrait, c. 1945.
        Photographer Bert Six
RIGHT: *The Other Love*, 1947, with David Niven

HUMPHREY BOGART

The essential Bogart has always been Rick, the expatriate café-owner of *Casablanca*; wounded but still stirred by Ingrid Bergman, he ultimately decides to place honour and self-possession above passion. In that role he became the blueprint of one of the screen's most powerful symbols of masculinity – the intelligent, sardonic man on the edge of conventional society, who pursues his own rigid code of principle and honour and rarely lowers his emotional guard because he foresees the chaos of letting go. In the early sixties, *Casablanca* was to become a cult movie and Bogart a cult hero. Bogie addicts, most of them too young to have seen the movie when it first came out, knew every single classic line: 'Here's looking at you, kid.' 'We'll always have Paris.' 'The problems of three little people don't amount to a hill o' beans in this crazy world.' It was an era of man-made evils – cold war, assassination, corruption, pollution – and the new generation was looking back for inspiration to the cynical, pessimistic hero of a piece of five-star romance.

Bogart was short and stocky, and was not a conventionally good-looking male: 'How can an ugly man be so handsome?' asked Marta Toren in *Sirocco*. Indeed Warners could not conceive of him as a heart-throb at all and for much of his career in the thirties, they projected only his tough-guy persona. He later claimed that of his first thirty-four pictures, he was shot in twelve, electrocuted or hanged in eight, and a jailbird in nine. Like Cagney he had an inimitable style of delivery perfectly suited to gangster roles; he spoke as though he were munching iron filings, with a faint and much imitated lisp. But his vulnerable toughness, detached chivalry and tantalizing blend of distance and intimacy also made him one of the great romantic heroes.

OPPOSITE: studio portrait, c. 1939.
ABOVE: *A Devil With Women*, 1930, with Mona Maris
LEFT: *High Sierra*, 1941, with Ida Lupino

111

Bogart had carved out a career as a romantic juvenile in the theatre, but was taken off to the West Coast by Fox, with whom he had made a handful of pictures, including *Up the River* in 1930, which marked the start of a lifelong friendship with its star, Spencer Tracy. However, Bogart was dropped by Fox and it was only in 1936, when Leslie Howard prevailed upon Warner Brothers to use Bogart (rather than Edward G. Robinson) for the screen role of Duke Mantee in *The Petrified Forest*, on the strength of his stage performance, that he established himself in Hollywood. His success won him a place in Warners' stable of gangsters and he appeared in a series of tough-guy films, of which the best were *San Quentin*, 1937, and Raoul Walsh's *They Drive by Night*, 1940.

Over the next five years, Bogart made some of his classic films. In 1941, he played the lonely, detached outsider in *High Sierra*, and appeared as Sam Spade in *The Maltese Falcon*. In 1940 he starred as Rick in *Casablanca*. Then, in 1944, he made *To Have and Have Not*, an adaptation of the Hemingway novel which featured a newcomer named Lauren Bacall. She was only twenty, he was forty-five; but they plunged into love and he got a divorce from his third wife — a volatile blonde named Mayo Methot who had always matched him drink for drink and punch for punch — to marry Bacall. Bogart and Bacall's crackling attraction for each other was immortalized in *The Big Sleep*, 1946, and *Key Largo*, 1948. The voltage of the scenes between Bogart and Bacall raises the question whether real-life lovers make better screen pairings. Certainly all their scenes are intriguing because of the real feeling between them. On the other hand, Bogart and Bergman also made a wonderful pairing — cynical, unwilling Rick, cold, hard and introspective, opposite soft, generous Ilsa,

ABOVE: *Casablanca*, 1942, with Ingrid Bergman
RIGHT: *Across the Pacific*, 1942, with Mary Astor

so open and vulnerable — and yet it is rumoured that Bogart was close to dislike of his co-star. But then, maybe that is what gave his final rejection of her an extra edge.

At a time when the general mood, politically as well as socially, was conservative, Bacall and Bogart were both vociferous in their support of Adlai Stevenson and the Democrats; also Bogart's private life featured some heavy drinking and well-documented pranks with Hollywood cronies. Nevertheless, he continued getting good parts and made some memorable films, notably *In a Lonely Place*, 1950, with Gloria Grahame, *The Treasure of the Sierra Madre*, 1948, *The Caine Mutiny*, 1954, and, with Katharine Hepburn, *The African Queen*, 1951, before he embarked on his battle against cancer of the oesophagus. His last film was *The Harder They Fall*, 1956, and he died in January 1957.

RIGHT: *Dead Reckoning*, 1947, with Lizabeth Scott

LAUREN BACALL

When Lauren Bacall instructed Bogart on how to whistle in her film debut, *To Have and Have Not*, 1944, something novel was happening. For over and above her husky voice, slinky figure and beautifully alert face, Bacall possessed an attitude that was definably new. It was as if this wisecracking nineteen-year-old had taken something from the Bogart mould and fashioned it for herself. Bacall looked, sounded, acted as if she belonged to no-one. It was a striking pose. Even Bogart looks faintly bemused as he purses his lips and lets out the most admiring whistle you'll ever hear.

Born in New York City, Bacall had been working as a model there until Howard Hawks' wife spotted her picture on the cover of 'Harper's Bazaar'. With no acting experience, she was coached intensively into her first performance. Yet in *To Have and Have Not* and *The Big Sleep*, 1946, Bogart and Bacall established a novel rapport of mutual self-respect which went against the grain of *film noir* relationships. Ladd and Lake were mere high-gloss figments of the imagination in comparison, while the William Powell–Myrna Loy partnership seemed like a relic of thirties conventionality. When Bogart and Bacall married in 1945, they seemed like a prototype for the perfect post-war couple: he was a growling, cynical optimist who'd seen it all; she was youthful but already world-weary, and wiser than her years.

Through *Dark Passage*, 1947, and *Key Largo*, 1948, they continued and developed that relationship. Bacall began to go her own way on screen from the early fifties, and took pride in refusing roles she considered unsuitable; Warners punished her several times by suspension. In *How to Marry a Millionaire*, 1953, she was a memorable gold digger opposite Marilyn Monroe and Betty Grable, and she

OPPOSITE: studio portrait, 1946.
Photographer Scotty Welbourne
RIGHT: publicity portrait for *The Big Sleep*, 1946,
with Humphrey Bogart.
Photographer John Engstead

took strong roles in *The Cobweb*, 1955, and *Written on the Wind*, 1956; but in general she seemed less than interested in most of her screen characters. Bogart died of cancer in 1957, and Bacall later married (and divorced) Jason Robards Jr.

None of Bacall's roles of the fifties seemed to fulfil her initial promise. The world was by then apparently made of plush, upholstered heroines asked only to giggle and get on with wearing out their consumer luxuries. Bacall's bleak, generous features stood out handsomely, but she never made the most of her uniqueness.

RIGHT: studio portrait, 1944.
Photographer Henry Waxman
BELOW: *Confidential Agent*, 1945, with
Charles Boyer

In her early career Lana Turner was billed variously, as the successor to Harlow, or perhaps Crawford; they said she would inherit the type of roles made famous by Loy or Colbert; or she was the forces' favourite pin-up, 'The Sweater Girl'. It was some time before this pneumatic blonde came into her own as the very epitome of a tinseltown movie star. Her plastic features and cantilevered frame could have been immaculately conceived in the famous Hollywood drugstore where she was by legend discovered; for Turner was the triumph of plucked-eyebrow-artifice over reality.

Turner began in bit-parts as a favourite of director Mervyn LeRoy, but soon graduated after *Dancing Co-Ed*, 1939, to bigger parts. MGM tried her out opposite their top male leads in *Dr*

Jekyll and Mr Hyde, 1941, with Spencer Tracy, in *Honky Tonk*, 1942, with Clark Gable, and in an early attempt at *film noir* opposite Robert Taylor, *Johnny Eager*, 1942. But her lack of training could not be disguised: every slight expression of grief seemed to swell to fever pitch, every smile of joy just missed bringing tears to her eyes. Only when she landed the part of the scheming wife Cora in Tay Garnett's *The Postman Always Rings Twice*, 1946, did she begin to show her peculiar genius. Her screen lover John Garfield was her polar opposite: ruggedly sincere, unashamedly working class, naturally simple. When she rolls her lipstick over towards him in the opening scene, his face registers surprise at this invitation to the world her character represents: a world of

money-lust, shameful passion, petty aspirations, a world which will shortly engulf them both.

There followed a run of hit movies, competition at MGM with Elizabeth Taylor and Ava Gardner, and then a breakthrough with a lead part in Vincente Minnelli's *The Bad and the Beautiful*, 1952, a seamy melodrama of Hollywood life in which Turner plays an ambitious, egotistical star-monster. She was very good at it. Her leading part in *Peyton Place*, 1958, came along after she had been dropped by MGM, but it brought her an Oscar nomination for her role as a suburban mother who

ABOVE: studio portrait, c. 1938
Photographer Laszlo Willinger

doesn't understand her daughter.

Some called her performance in the witness stand that same year her best ever: she was defending her daughter who had killed Turner's lover, gangster Johnny Stompanato, with a bread-knife. The case brought revelations of torrid sex secrets, making front-page news for months, and it prompted producer Ross Hunter to select her for Douglas Sirk's remake of *Imitation of Life*, 1958, in which she plays an ambitious star whose adopted half-caste daughter goes off the rails. She was highly convincing as the manipulative

RIGHT: *The Postman Always Rings Twice*, 1946, with John Garfield
BELOW: publicity portrait for *The Rains of Ranchipur*, 1955, with Richard Burton

career woman whose life of material comfort conceals a tawdry and un-giving emotional life. For some it is merely cheap melodrama; but as Turner's own life had shown, it was that potent sense of disaster about to emerge from the celluloid American dream that made her performance so tearfully moving. It was all so fitting for a poor small-time girl who had been shot to stardom, whose real-life romances and seven marriages included a bandleader, a gangster, a playboy-millionaire, an actor and one ex-Tarzan, Lex Barker.

LEFT: off set *Diane*, 1955
BELOW: *Johnny Eager*, 1942, with Robert Taylor

SPENCER TRACY

Spencer Tracy first appeared – on Broadway – as a robot, but graduated to respected eminence playing flawed though fundamentally good characters; men of strength and integrity who represented American normality. Craggy and dignified but also sharp-tongued, he was the son of a truck salesman and had originally intended to go into the priesthood, and his casting in some of his most memorable roles turned on his sense of Catholic integrity. He once said his face was 'as plain as a barn door' but thanks to his on/off screen pairing with Hepburn, he also had a strong romantic image.

Tracy made his film debut for John Ford in *Up the River* in 1930, and although he was successful for Fox, he was not the most pliant of actors and was sacked in 1935. Promptly signed by MGM, he made two outstanding films in the next few years, winning two Oscars: the first in 1937 for *Captains Courageous* and the second the following year for his performance as Father Flanagan, reforming Mickey Rooney in *Boys Town*.

His glorious screen partnership with Katharine Hepburn began in *Woman of the Year*, 1942, and they went on to make wonderful comedies, playing with the notion of contest between masculine and feminine wiles. One of the best examples was as the married lawyers in *Adam's Rib*, a film which gave a very representative view of masculinity in the forties, in which either of the sexes may outsmart each other, but the man is always on top in the bedroom. Off screen, Tracy had a lifelong romantic friendship with Hepburn, but he never divorced his wife, Louise Treadwell, and the relationship was treated discreetly by the gossip columnists of the day. Tracy emerged from the retirement caused by his poor health, to make *Guess Who's Coming to Dinner* in 1967 with Hepburn; although obviously extremely ill, he carried on working on the production and died only shortly after its completion.

ABOVE: *Woman of the Year*, 1942, with Katharine Hepburn
OPPOSITE: publicity portrait, c. 1931

KATHARINE HEPBURN

The prevailing wisdom that Katharine Hepburn was never considered conventionally beautiful seems perverse. Certainly her high cheekbones, piercing eyes and flashing smile are of a different order to both Garbo's exoticism or Harlow's dimestore platinum blonde, if they are taken as the two extremes of thirties glamour. Hepburn is uniquely East Coast establishment, the proud and confident daughter of a wealthy Connecticut family, an actress whose Bryn Mawr College accent sounded a novel note in Hollywood. Certainly her quality of refined intelligence belied a reputation as a mere

OPPOSITE: studio portrait, 1936.
        Photographer Ernest A. Bachrach
RIGHT: *The Philadelphia Story*, 1940, with
        James Stewart
BELOW: *Sylvia Scarlett*, 1935, with Brian Aherne

'beauty'. But perhaps the reason was simpler even than this: here was a fêted Broadway actress whose early movie roles won her popular success, critical acclaim and a brace of Oscar nominations, as well as rumours of an engagement to mogul Howard Hughes. It may just have been too galling for Hollywood gossips to admit that, with all this, Hepburn was actually *beautiful* too.

The movie colony's reaction to her was certainly peculiar. Her earliest starring roles for RKO were all hits: *A Bill of Divorcement*, 1932, *Morning Glory* (for which she won an Oscar) and *Little Women*, both 1933. Roles like

LEFT: *Undercurrent*, 1946, with Robert Taylor
BELOW: *Bringing Up Baby*, 1938

ABOVE: studio portrait, 1936.
Photographer Ernest A. Bachrach

the aviatrix *Christopher Strong*, 1933, and the androgynous *Sylvia Scarlett*, 1935, established her as an unorthodox and independent actress with the same scornful disdain for Hollywood etiquette that she had had for Broadway etiquette in an earlier stage of her career. Yet the prestigious *Quality Street*, 1937, was a failure, and not even her classic comic lead opposite Cary Grant in *Bringing Up Baby*, 1938, could bring her back to favour. Her RKO period came to an end, and, like Joan Crawford, she was labelled 'box office poison' by exhibitors — as if no-one had ever laughed at the sight of her trying to control a leopard on a leash in one of Hepburn and Grant's more bizarre comic moments.

The Philadelphia Story, 1940, brought her back to Hollywood and MGM with an Oscar nomination, a

smash hit and a mint of money, for on her return to Broadway she had starred in and picked up the film rights to this hugely popular comedy. As an elegant heiress opposite James Stewart and Cary Grant, Hepburn excels at sophisticated banter, alternately as flirtatious as a kitten and stuffily severe. She was in her prime. When MGM teamed her for the first time with Spencer Tracy in *Woman of the Year*, 1942, their chemistry was immediately apparent. They were complete opposites. Tracy appeared bullish, instinctive, quietly sly; Hepburn was strong-willed, fiery, cleverly talkative. They excelled in battles of the sexes, and transformed the on-screen duels of *State of the Union*, 1948, *Adam's Rib*, 1949, and *Pat and Mike*, 1952, into an off-screen relationship of lasting affection. They never married (Tracy would not insist

on a divorce from his wife), but their partnership was an open secret for the rest of their lives.

Hepburn managed both to astonish Bogart in *The African Queen*, 1951, and win another Oscar nomination. Although her liberated image now tended towards overtly spinsterish roles, films like *Summer Madness*, 1955, *The Rainmaker*, 1956, *Suddenly Last Summer*, 1959, and especially *Long Day's Journey Into Night*, 1962, all benefited from her presence. If the fifties was a busy decade for her, she spent five years from 1962 away from stage or screen, nursing a dying father and seriously ill Tracy. The famous pair returned for *Guess Who's Coming to Dinner*, 1967, Tracy's last film. It won her an Oscar, as did *The Lion in Winter*, 1968, with Peter O'Toole, and later *On Golden Pond*, 1981, with Henry Fonda. She encouraged sympathy and admiration from both critics and audience, even if her acting had long since drifted into mannerism.

Nobody cared, since Hepburn had not only consistently justified her position at the top of her profession, but had also come to be recognized as a truly emancipated woman, one who was just as in tune with the post-sixties world of Jane Fonda and Vanessa Redgrave as with the Hollywood establishment of which she was so much a part. Her mother had been a suffragette and early supporter of birth control, and some of that tough, New England-style radicalism managed to permeate the tinseltown glamour in which Hepburn was perpetually shrouded. As the jaded sophisticate, daring aviatrix, screwball comic, shrewd careerist or battling spinster, Hepburn never let go of that inheritance. All that, and beautiful too.

ABOVE: studio portrait, 1941.
         Photographer Clarence Sinclair Bull
RIGHT: publicity portrait for *Without Love*, 1945,
         with Spencer Tracy.
         Photographer Clarence Sinclair Bull
OPPOSITE: studio portrait, 1938.
         Photographer Laszlo Willinger

Darryl F. Zanuck called Tyrone Power 'the truest, handsomest, best of the lot'. He was certainly nice and very beautiful, with reasonable acting abilities which might perhaps have been allowed to develop if his charm and good looks had not kept him in the romantic swashbuckler mould. For a decade from the late thirties, he was Fox's major box-office star, versatile enough to lead in musicals and Westerns as well as costume epics. His finest performance was as the nimble hero disguised as an effeminate fop in *The Mark of Zorro*, 1940, which ends with the famous beauty-and-the-beast sword duel with baddie Basil Rathbone. After the war, Power took on more serious roles, but never with the same success. 'I'm sick of all these knight in shining armour parts,' he once said, 'I want to do something worthwhile like plays and films that have something to say.' Unfortunately, though, his public simply did not want to see him in unsympathetic roles, and he was condemned to swash and buckle in costume dramas for most of his career.

Son of a matinée idol and silents actor, Tyrone Power Sr, and great grandson of a famous thespian of the same name, Power Jr went on stage in his teens, then graduated through bit parts to his first big success in *Lloyds of London*, 1937, and took the title role in *Jesse James*. His talent for costume parts was established in *The Rains Came*, 1939, in which he played the Indian surgeon prince fancied by Myrna Loy. These were followed by *The Mark of Zorro* along with other dashing costume performances such as the pirate opposite Maureen O'Hara in *The Black Swan*, 1942, the wronged heir helping to conquer Mexico in *Captain from Castile*, 1947, and the Renaissance adventurer in *Prince of Foxes*, 1949.

After war service he found a more interesting role as a Somerset Maugham drop-out in *The Razor's Edge*, 1946, and won critical acclaim as a carnival barker turned fake mind-

reader in the *film noir Nightmare Alley*, 1947, but failed to escape his pre-war mould and returned to staightforward adventure heroes in various genres. However, in Billy Wilder's courtroom drama, *Witness for the Prosecution*, 1958, he played a man on trial for murdering Norma Varden, with only one witness – wife Marlene Dietrich –

able to provide an alibi. The same year he died after a heart attack on set; in suitably heroic style he had been duelling with George Sanders during the filming of *Solomon and Sheba*. Tragically, three months after his death, his wife, Linda Christian, gave birth to the son he had so desperately wanted.

OPPOSITE ABOVE: *Blood and Sand*, 1941, with Rita Hayworth
OPPOSITE BELOW: *Ladies in Love*, 1936, with Loretta Young
ABOVE: *The Black Swan*, 1942

MERLE OBERON

Whenever Merle Oberon is seen as Cathy in *Wuthering Heights*, 1939, she never leaves a dry eye in the house. Opposite Laurence Olivier's Heathcliff, she seems to ebb and swell with passion until her heart breaks; and it is only after seeing it many times that one begins to notice the Californian sets, the truncated and perfunctory script and, indeed, Oberon's own weaknesses. But no matter that her speech is polite and characterless: her frail physique and imploring eyes do more on screen than many more talented thespians could manage.

Born in India, Oberon was to carve out a peripatetic career for herself on both sides of the Atlantic. In England in 1933 producer and future husband Alexander Korda first gave her a break with the part of Anne Boleyn in *The Private Life of Henry VIII*. After a lead opposite Leslie Howard in the extravagant costumes of *The Scarlet Pimpernel*, 1935, she was in demand everywhere; but a bad accident set a temporary halt to her career and a permanent one to Korda's *I, Claudius*, which she was making at the time. Though Korda's influence guided her throughout the thirties and early forties (they divorced in 1945), she was much more than his successful protégé. In 1935 Korda had sold a share of her contract to Sam Goldwyn, and thereafter she commuted between London and Hollywood. Perhaps Korda's predilection for historical pomp inhibited her transition to more modern circumstances, for certainly her contemporary roles left much to be desired. Her screen appearances in the fifties were sporadic, and even by the time she made *Berlin Express* in 1948, her career was visibly on the decline. Her previous associations with more grandiose leading men made a square-jawed *homme ordinaire* like Dana Andrews look like a demotion.

OPPOSITE: studio portrait, 1944.
      Photographer Robert W. Coburn
ABOVE: *The Scarlet Pimpernel*, 1935, with Leslie Howard
LEFT: *Beloved Enemy*, 1936, with David Niven

ARLETTY

As the central romantic figure of Marcel Carné's epic *Les Enfants du paradis*, 1944, Arletty occupies a similar role in French lore to Scarlett O'Hara in America: a woman desired by all men, fickle and impulsive, deeply passionate yet doomed to unhappiness. Her role as Garance, the courtesan, is the pivot around which this sprawling, magnificent movie turns, as she is pursued by four lovers – Jean-Louis Barrault, Pierre Brasseur, Louis Salou and Marcel Herrand. She sustains the film without swamping it, a performance of precisely judged nuances that has grown in stature even after its huge contemporary success.

Arletty (born Léonie Bathiat) had already appeared in other classics, among them Carné's *Le Jour se lève*, 1939, and *Les Visiteurs du soir*, 1942, in which she is a world-weary heroine in a haunting landscape that captured the uncertainty of these years. She was in her forties by then and reaching the peak of a long career spent until 1931 in the music hall and on stage. The aura of an older woman is accentuated by the complete assurance which she brings to all her performances. She was able, for instance, to dominate the screen version of Jean-Paul Sartre's *Huis clos*, 1954, as a tormenting lesbian, seemingly terrifying her fellow actors. Overall, she has no match in the American cinema as an actress, since her persona is mature and adult, and she is expert at portraying sombre emotions and passions unmistakably born out of real-life experience. After the liberation of Paris she was briefly jailed for collaboration with the Germans because of a love affair with a Nazi officer, and she has done very little on stage or screen since the early sixties.

OPPOSITE: *Les Visiteurs du soir*, 1942
ABOVE: *Les Enfants du paradis*, 1944, with Jean-Louis Barrault
LEFT: *Le Jour se lève*, 1939

JEAN GABIN

Jean Gabin made his name in the thirties in France as a tough, doomed, ugly-beautiful anti-hero, before maturing into Spencer Tracy-type roles of vigorous seniority; many of his qualities foreshadowed Belmondo and Depardieu – working-class ruggedness, honesty and integrity. He survived all the changing fashions in the cinema and, astonishingly, was still his country's most popular actor at the end of the sixties.

The son of music hall entertainers, he started work as a labourer before entering show business as a dancer with the Folies-Bergère. His first film, *Chacun Sa Chance*, 1930, was followed by fine performances over the next decade in classics of the French cinema like *Pépé le Moko*, playing a Parisian king of crime who comes out for love of a woman and is slaughtered by police, and *La Grande Illusion*, in which he was a working-class officer in a First World War prison camp. In 1939 he made *Le Jour Se Lève*, playing a factory worker who, with justification, kills lecher Jules Berry and then waits in a hotel room for the police to come and get him.

A year later, Gabin decided to try his luck in Hollywood but he did not transplant successfully and returned to Europe to fight with the Free French. His forties and fifties pictures with such directors as Carné, Becker and Renoir, were consistently good and in 1958 he played Simenon's inspector hero for the first time in *Maigret Tend Un Piège*. By the time he died in 1976, he had become a national institution.

ABOVE: *La Bête Humaine*, 1938, with Simone Simon

OPPOSITE: studio portrait, 1945. Photographer Ernest A. Bachrach

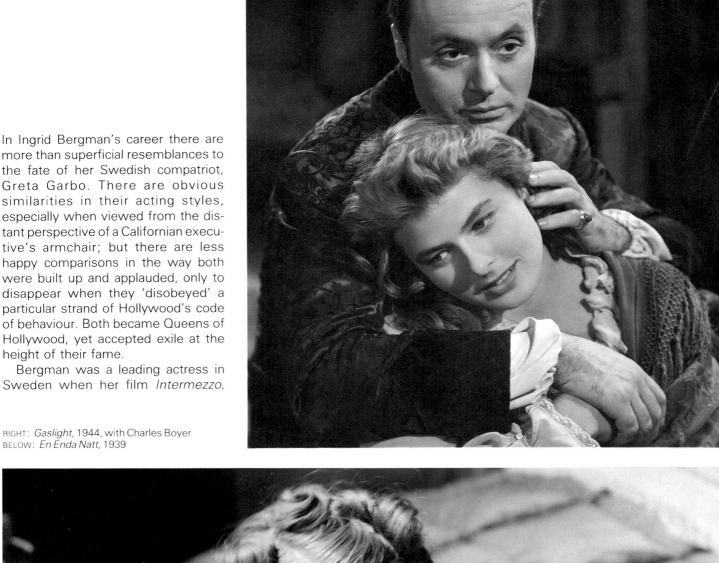

In Ingrid Bergman's career there are more than superficial resemblances to the fate of her Swedish compatriot, Greta Garbo. There are obvious similarities in their acting styles, especially when viewed from the distant perspective of a Californian executive's armchair; but there are less happy comparisons in the way both were built up and applauded, only to disappear when they 'disobeyed' a particular strand of Hollywood's code of behaviour. Both became Queens of Hollywood, yet accepted exile at the height of their fame.

Bergman was a leading actress in Sweden when her film *Intermezzo*,

RIGHT: *Gaslight*, 1944, with Charles Boyer
BELOW: *En Enda Natt*, 1939

1936, came to the attention of producer David O. Selznick. At great expense he imported her to Hollywood, where he promoted her as a great natural beauty who, like some seedling plucked from a Scandinavian forest, needed no make-up to be fully appreciated. Her Hollywood debut was in a remake of *Intermezzo*, co-starring Leslie Howard and released in 1939. After that her career zigzagged, for she was personally contracted to Selznick and he was taking a break from movie-making. Loaned out to various studios she played diverse roles, from a tarty barmaid in *Dr Jekyll and Mr Hyde*, 1941, to a Hedy Lamarr

LEFT: *Casablanca*, 1942, with Humphrey Bogart
BELOW: *Spellbound*, 1945

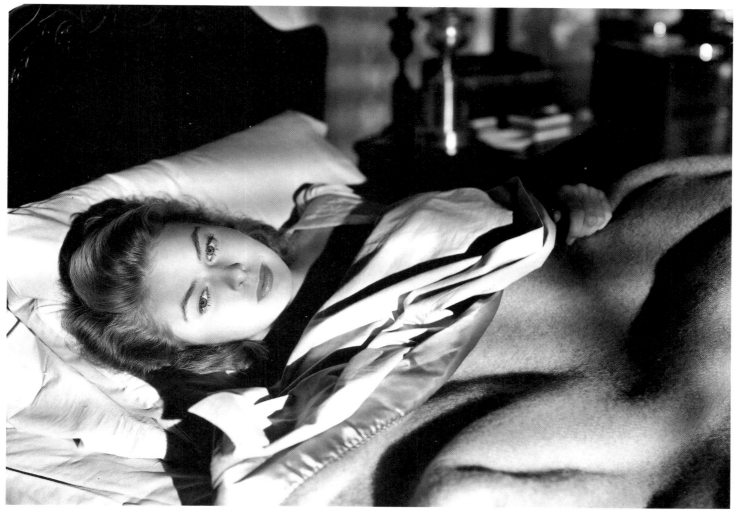

replacement opposite Bogart in *Casablanca*, 1942, in which she is torn between love for her old flame Rick and loyalty to her husband. In a potentially banal setting, she proved her talent for the understatement of intense emotion. Selznick persuaded Hemingway to endorse her as the lead in *For Whom the Bell Tolls*, 1943; and she really came into her own with *Gaslight*, 1944, for which she won an Oscar for her interpretation of a wife slowly going insane under the tormenting of her husband, played by Charles Boyer.

From then on, she seemed to do little wrong, especially for Hitchcock in *Spellbound*, 1945, with Gregory Peck, and in *Notorious*, 1946, opposite Cary Grant and Claude Rains, her last films under contract to Selznick. In *Notorious* she played a spy engaged in undercover work, apparently cast off by Grant in a callous denial of their love, and in Hitchcock's erotically long, lingering shots Bergman is magnetic. *The Bells of St Mary's*, 1945, with Bing Crosby, didn't quite hit the same standard, although it was her biggest box office success to date and earned her an Oscar nomination. Nothing, it seemed, could displace her as the nation's top dramatic star.

Except a scandal. After *Joan of Arc*, 1948, she left Hollywood for Italy, where she fell in love with movie director Roberto Rossellini and bore his child out of wedlock (they married in 1950). Vilified, denounced and virtually blacklisted by the American press for her sins, her powerful performances in his *Stromboli*, 1949, *Europa '51*, 1951, and *Viaggio in Italia*, 1953, were almost ignored in the USA. After Hollywood's careful artifice, these films were raw and compellingly rough, with plots more angst-laden and bleak than her usual happy endings. Nothing detracted from the strength of her emotions, and her charisma shone through the

LEFT: *For Whom the Bell Tolls*, 1943, with Gary Cooper

films' often sketchy characterizations.

It was said that American audiences only loved her when she was playing a *good* woman. However incredible this puritanism may seem for the supposedly rocking 'n' rolling fifties, Bergman was on the receiving end of it for many years. She was only publicly forgiven with an Oscar for her part in the American production, *Anastasia*, 1956, in which she played the pretender to the Tsar's throne. This and another noble weepie, *The Inn of the Sixth Happiness*, 1958, were saturated with suffering in adversity; and they carried a masochistic undertow to them which tilted her performances towards mawkish sentiment. In that same year her marriage to Rossellini was dissolved, and she later married a Swedish stage producer.

Like Garbo, Bergman possessed the ability to suggest great depth of emotion without histrionics; and it is that ability which so many American actresses have lacked. She knew the secret of hinting at inner terror without resorting to outward babble, and of projecting that uncannily clearly on screen. But unlike Garbo, she seemed devoid of a lasting independence from men: she could suffer in silence, but always seemed to believe that her characters' happiness depended ultimately on being one half of a partnership. This sense possibly made her movies more interesting dramas, but perhaps detracted from her eventual stature as a star; for in that slight weakness, she compromised her mythical status and descended to the all-too-recognizable reality that most of us inhabit.

ABOVE: publicity portrait for *Saratoga Trunk*, 1945.
Photographer Scotty Welbourne
RIGHT: *Stromboli*, 1949

OVER: Marlon Brando, studio portrait, c. 1949

THE FIFTIES

GREGORY PECK

Peck is happier being a monument to human decency than he is as a sex symbol, and it was once said that he was 'wooden to the core'. The trouble with Peck's leading men is that since they are almost invariably required to personify such worthy characteristics as integrity, sincerity and liberal thought, he often comes through with almost no spark of life at all. But nobody could accuse him of being just a handsome bonehead in *To Kill a Mockingbird*, as Atticus Finch, a small-town lawyer defending a black man accused of rape; or as the high-principled officer in *The Guns of Navarone*, or in the early *Gentleman's Agreement*, as the journalist posing as a Jew in order to probe American anti-Semitism. While it is true that he rarely inflames us with passion, he makes his best characters vivid through the moral conflicts that nag them.

Exempt from military service through a long-standing spine injury, Peck became an almost instant war-time star in an industry deprived of many of its leading men. He had spent most of his childhood with relatives after his parents had divorced, and enrolled at the Neighborhood Play-house in New York after studying at the University of California. After work-ing on Broadway, he headed for Holly-wood in 1943 and made his debut in *Days of Glory*, 1944. In a career span-ning more than thirty years, he has brought a heavyweight presence to films of almost every genre: drama, Westerns, action and war movies, even romantic comedy. Some of them have been exceptional. His early films included *The Keys of the Kingdom*, 1945, *The Yearling*, 1946, *Gentle-man's Agreement*, 1947, and *The Gun-fighter*, 1950. However, he has also looked beyond self-sacrificing and saintly roles, as in *Duel in the Sun*, 1946, and *Moby Dick* in 1956.

OPPOSITE: studio portrait, 1945.
      Photographer Ernest Bachrach
ABOVE: *Spellbound*, 1945, with Ingrid Bergman
RIGHT: *Duel in the Sun*, 1946, with
      Jennifer Jones

143

Peck's first marriage ended in 1953; he met his second wife, Véronique, a French journalist, when she was despatched to interview him for 'Paris Match'. Now one of the grand old men of the cinema, he has served as President of the Academy of Motion Picture Arts and Sciences. He is also associated with many charitable and political causes and retains his off-screen liberal links: a few years back he discovered that he occupied a prominent position on Richard Nixon's list of dangerous enemies.

RIGHT: publicity portrait for *The Great Sinner*, 1949
BELOW: *Roman Holiday*, 1953, with Audrey Hepburn

On one of the posters for *Gilda*, 1946, Rita Hayworth poses in a black evening gown, elbow-length black gloves encasing her arms, drawing coolly on a cigarette. It was an image from the famous sequence 'Put the Blame On Mame', a seductive striptease which entices Glenn Ford and almost every other male in the audience into raptures for her. But artists' impressions of that image turn her into a wisp of smoke, a mirage from some magical lamp rather than a real woman. It was perhaps fair licence. For Hayworth was not so much the missing link between Harlow and Monroe, as is often claimed, but rather a unique personification of fantasies which crystallized around her figure in the mid-forties. She was a heightened version of a *femme fatale*, worthy of infinite sacrifice and casual betrayal. She was a reincarnation of World War One's Theda Bara, restyled for World War Two GIs into an image of unparalleled beauty which seemed in the end to destroy her. 'Every man I knew', she once said, 'had fallen in love with Gilda and wakened with me.'

She was born Margarita Cansino, daughter of a Spanish dancer, and related by marriage to Ginger Rogers. A teenage dancer and bit-part movie actress, she did not really emerge from the shadows until she was twenty-one when her first husband got her a contract at Columbia. Reincarnated as Hayworth, now a dyed redhead with a hairline raised by electrolysis, she got her first break with Howard Hawks' *Only Angels Have Wings*, 1939. Then she settled into a niche as the 'other woman' in *Strawberry Blonde, Affectionately Yours*, and most triumphantly opposite Tyrone Power in *Blood and Sand*, all 1941. She also kept up her talent as a highly effective dancer, partnering Fred Astaire in *You'll Never Get Rich*, 1941, and *You Were Never Lovelier*, 1942, and co-starring with Victor Mature in *My Gal Sal*, 1942, and Gene Kelly in *Cover Girl*, 1944.

RIGHT: publicity portrait for *Gilda*, 1946.
Photographer Robert W. Coburn

But *Gilda* was the image that stayed
with her. Opposite Glenn Ford her
agile face, full lips and flowing locks
glowed like luminous jewels; he was
subtly chosen to contrast, a bullish,
squat, almost ugly partner, as earth-
bound as any man in the audience
might feel when confronted with her
charms. Orson Welles, the second of
five husbands, came closest to re-
creating that effect in his dazzling *The
Lady from Shanghai*, 1948, filmed as
they were filing for divorce. Hayworth
in the title role is mysterious and
predatory, deviously cruel; her hair

RIGHT: publicity portrait for *You'll Never Get Rich*,
      1941, with Fred Astaire.
      Photographer A. L. 'Whitey' Schaefer
BELOW: publicity portrait for *The Lady from
      Shanghai*, 1948, with Orson Welles.
      Photographer Robert W. Coburn

was chopped off and dyed blonde for the part. It is a bitter, hateful, but erotically powerful movie. In a posed still from the famous shoot-out in the hall of mirrors, Welles grasps her close to him. She tilts her head back and seems to mock him, as if he is only holding her reflection in his arms.

It was perhaps her key role. It was in any case the last that she was able to play with genuine passion. A well-publicized but stormy two-year marriage to Prince Aly Khan in 1949 lasted long enough to wreck her association with Columbia and apparently to kill off the spark which brought her alive on screen. She was soon pleading with

LEFT: *The Loves of Carmen*, 1948, with Glenn Ford
BELOW: *Affair in Trinidad*, 1952, with Glenn Ford

Harry Cohn to allow her to return to her old studio, and she went on to earn herself a lot of money but little satisfaction. As if playing safe, the studio cast her in roles as *Salome*, 1953, and *Miss Sadie Thompson*, 1953, and these settled her into a run-of-the-mill Hollywood slot that contrasted sadly with her position for almost a decade on some sort of Olympian plinth. Many movies followed, but only *Pal Joey*, 1957, with Frank Sinatra could really claim to be anything approaching special.

Hayworth started out as the very epitome of glamour, a perfect incarnation of a Hollywood 'love goddess' who ruled the world. During the war, her 'Life' magazine pictures were printed in millions and despatched to troops on the front line. To them, she was a symbol – and this was more true of her than of many who have acquired that label – of a far-off world of sex, satin sheets, nightclubs, cigarette smoke, booze, and fast, dangerous women on the dance floor. But as the post-war world stabilized into one of

family duties and television, her purpose and essence seemed to evaporate, much like the wisp of smoke that had symbolized her most famous role. As the years went by, her private life became a protracted story of self-destruction and personal tragedy.

ABOVE: publicity portrait for *Salome*, 1953, with Stewart Granger.
Photographer Robert W. Coburn

JAMES MASON

James Mason was rarely the straight-forward gentleman he appeared: under the surface there usually lurked fatal flaws of weakness or cruelty, whether he was a romantic leading man, an avuncular relation or military leader. His talent – he provided Judy Garland with the best support she ever had in *A Star is Born*, 1954, and brought immense skill to the totally contrasting role of Humbert Humbert in *Lolita*, 1962 – has invariably compensated for the mediocre films which have punctuated his Hollywood career.

Born in the north of England, he went on the stage after studying architecture at Cambridge University. He then went into British films and became one of the strongest male stars by the mid-forties, notably as the sadistic Marquis, whipping Margaret Lockwood to death in *The Man in Grey*, 1943, the vicious Lord Manderstoke in *Fanny by Gaslight*, 1944, and the cruel guardian in *The Seventh Veil*, 1945. In his Hollywood films of the fifties, which were very variable, Mason often played more obviously villainous heroes; his notable performances of those years included Rommel in *The Desert Fox*, 1951, and *The Desert Rats*, 1953, the spy in *Five Fingers*, 1952, and the villain of Hitchcock's *North by Northwest*, 1959.

LEFT: studio portrait, 1950.
       Photographer Ted Reed

Judy Garland always retained the magic that rubbed off from *The Wizard of Oz*, 1939. Beautiful, fresh and appealing as Mickey Rooney's sweetheart in *Strike Up the Band*, 1940, it was somehow appalling that, by the time of *A Star is Born*, 1954, she should be so visibly racked by the real traumas and cracked lines of adulthood. Her persona was always balanced precariously between those two extremes. The tragic story of her reliance on drugs and the collapse of her career is well known; and yet she achieved some of the purest screen definitions of romance.

Meet Me in St Louis, 1944, is, of course, a sweet-toothed reminder of her days as a juvenile hoofer *à la* Shirley Temple. But *The Pirate*, 1947, with Gene Kelly is a dashingly exuberant parody of swashbuckling folk, in which Garland's Technicolor dreams of love with her phantom pirate make one almost giddy with colour, movement and sheer energy. But it was a little-remembered movie, *The Clock*, 1945, also directed by her second husband Vincente Minnelli, in which she gave one of her strongest performances. Unlike many of the movies for which Garland is famous, it is a real-life fairy-tale filmed in black and white, without the benefit of songs. It is Garland who provides the film's soaring heights and intensity. She plays a young girl who falls in love with soldier Robert Walker on twenty-four-hour leave in New York. The panic in her eyes when she thinks she has lost him is unforgettable: it brings memories of how in her best music her heart seems to swell until it might burst, and is reminiscent of the sense of fear and elation that pervades a vintage silent like *Sunrise*. Garland may have made better movies, but she never had a stronger sense of hope.

OPPOSITE: publicity portrait for *The Clock*, 1945, with Robert Walker
ABOVE: *Words and Music*, 1948, with Mickey Rooney
LEFT: studio portrait, 1957. Photographer John Engstead

BURT LANCASTER

Legend has it that Lancaster was discovered in an elevator by a stage producer who thought he was an actor and invited him to read for a Broadway part: He not only got the part, but also lasted long enough in the role to be spotted by Hollywood talent scouts. A graceful, swaggering chunk of a man whose compelling physical presence is combined with intriguing tenderness, he grew up on Manhattan's rough East Harlem area and won an athletics scholarship to college, but left to become a circus acrobat. In his first movie, *The Killers*, 1946, he was a hunk in an undershirt waiting for his killers; it made him a major star and he went on to appear in some notable fun thrillers, including the swashbuckling *The Crimson Pirate*, 1962.

Other major films include *From Here to Eternity*, 1953, *Sweet Smell of Success*, 1957, and *The Birdman of Alcatraz*, for which he won a Venice Festival award in 1962. But he has also come to be appreciated as an extremely sensitive actor. He won an Oscar for *Elmer Gantry*, 1960, and displayed intriguing tenderness and a forceful sense of oppressed power and passion in two electrifying performances for Visconti; first in *The Leopard*, 1963, and then as an aging professor confronting homosexuality in *Conversation Piece*, 1974.

One of the first modern actors to set up a production company, he still appears in major films, although increasingly in character roles, still as strapping and vital as ever.

OPPOSITE: publicity portrait for *The Killers*, 1946
ABOVE: *Criss Cross*, 1948, with Yvonne de Carlo

AUDREY HEPBURN

With her doe-eyed charm and petite figure, Audrey Hepburn was a startlingly novel kind of beauty for the early fifties. Instead of buxom, blonde and giggling, she was slender, boyish and modest, with a *naïveté* which did not rule out sophistication. She became the first *gamine* to be accepted as overpoweringly chic, and opened up a niche later occupied by figures as diverse as Jean Seberg and Twiggy. It wasn't that Hepburn was a brilliant actress, or possessed a forceful personality. It was more that when the camera caught her face in close-up, everyone held their breath: she was simply so photogenic that everyone fell in love with her.

Ballet-trained, a model and bit-part movie actress, Hepburn was filming in the South of France when she met the great writer Colette. It was Colette who offered her the title role in the Broadway adaptation of her novel 'Gigi'; and from this Hepburn walked into *Roman Holiday*, 1953, as the young princess with whom Gregory Peck falls in love. She won an Academy Award for her role, proving to those who doubted that Hollywood could still be moved by novelty and freshness. She won another nomination for her next role in Billy Wilder's *Sabrina*, 1954, with Bogart and William Holden, and then played Natasha in King Vidor's ambitious *War and Peace*, 1956, opposite her new husband, Mel Ferrer. But it was *Funny Face*, 1957,

which best defined her qualities. She played a young model groomed by Fred Astaire for stardom in Stanley Donen's stylish version of the Gershwin musical, and, from photographer Richard Avedon's credits sequence onwards, her appeal was clear. Hepburn did not have to act so much as *be*: her face could register emotion simply by a blank stare.

She continued to have hits, and *Breakfast at Tiffany's*, 1961, brought her yet more admirers; but she seemed to have lost the freshness

ABOVE: publicity portrait for *Sabrina*, 1954.
Photographer Bud Fraker
OPPOSITE: publicity portrait for *Funny Face*, 1957.
Photographer Richard Avedon

which had been so surprising eight years before. Her role as Eliza Doolittle in *My Fair Lady*, 1964, seemed to show her artistic dilemma. She was indeed fine as the guttersnipe taken in by Pygmalion (the elderly Rex Harrison); but she was chosen over Julie Andrews because she was a 'safe' box office bet, and the 'safeness' of her performances was becoming all too evident. After *Two for the Road*, 1966, and *Wait Until Dark*, 1967, produced by Ferrer, and with five Oscar nominations to her credit, Hepburn went into semi-retirement with her second husband, and left her vintage fifties portraits to speak for themselves.

RIGHT: studio portrait, c. 1954.
     Photographer Bud Fraker
BELOW: publicity portrait for *Breakfast at*
     Tiffany's, 1961, with George Peppard
OPPOSITE: studio portrait, 1950.
     Photographer Bud Fraker

Charlton Heston's strapping, rough-hewn physique, sonorous voice and the intense, slightly tragic cast of his expression were part of a hulking screen presence that never got lost among the spectacular scenery, special effects and noisy battles that always seem to surround him. His strongest and sexiest role was as a Mexican drugs cop in Welles's *Touch of Evil*, 1958, with its steamy, exotic atmosphere, but the fans preferred to see him as beefcake in big-budget costume epics. He launched into them with *The Ten Commandments*, 1956, in which he doubled as Moses and the voice of God, won an Oscar for his gigantic portrayal of legendary hero *Ben-Hur*, 1959, and followed it up with an equally dominating performance as *El Cid*, 1961. In *The War Lord*, 1965, he was cast in the romantic hero mould as a medieval knight, but *Khartoum*, 1966, took him back to the desert and gave him the opportunity to explore a more complex character, General Gordon. During the sixties, his kind of mythic hero went out of fashion and he began to tackle different kinds of roles, shedding his heroic persona for the illiterate cowboy who didn't wash too often in *Will Penny*, 1968, taking on Shakespeare in the British *Julius Caesar*, 1970, and behaving nobly in disaster spectaculars like *Earthquake* and *Airport 1975*.

ABOVE: *Ben-Hur*, 1959
LEFT: *Touch of Evil*, 1958, with Janet Leigh
OPPOSITE: publicity portrait for *The Killers*, 1946.
Photographer Ray Jones

Ava Gardner was a 'Hemingway woman': strong-willed, impetuous, magnetically sensual, a beauty who seemed at home among admiring men, but who never seemed to give in too easily to anyone. She was a throwback to Hemingway's world of tough-guy mystique, which seemed to bore her as much as it did her more youthful audiences. In a famous interview with columnist Rex Reed in the sixties, she looked back over her career and was blunt in assessing her achievements: 'Hell, baby, after twenty-five years in this business, if all you've got to show for it is *Mogambo* and *The Hucksters* you might as well give up.' On that evidence she was probably her own best scriptwriter, and her glamorous public persona as a late 1940s rival to Hayworth – 'The World's Most Exciting Animal' as one publicist would have it – was a reluctant achievement, a sop to the powers-that-be. She had grown from a nineteen-year-old MGM contract player at $50 per week back in 1941 to a wealthy jet-setting woman of the world, and she played that role to the hilt. In between she made short-lived marriages to Mickey Rooney, bandleader Artie Shaw, and Frank Sinatra. With its front-page quarrels, that last romance probably had more Hollywood-style drama and tragedy in it than most of her movies. And at times, she seemed to know as much.

Until 1946 she had been used to years of bit-parts and fifth-billing, and then she donned black satin dress and gloves for publicity for her new movie, *The Killers*. She exuded just the right aura of sultry elegance as a *femme fatale* opposite another promising newcomer, Burt Lancaster, and she contrived an attractive but laconic laziness that might have been caught from Robert Mitchum. It was an intelligent version of a Hemingway story,

ABOVE: publicity portrait for *The Killers*, 1946, with Burt Lancaster. Photographer Ray Jones
RIGHT: *Mogambo*, 1953, with Clark Gable

and it established her as a star; movies like *The Hucksters*, 1947, opposite Gable and Deborah Kerr followed. But it was not until she starred in *My Forbidden Past*, 1951, as a Southern belle opposite Mitchum himself, that her particular talent for the don't-give-a-damn look was again required.

She was most often cast as some paradoxical monument to her own beauty. She was required to be suitably mythical in the surrealistic *Pandora and the Flying Dutchman*, 1951, and played the half-caste lead in *Show Boat*, 1951 in which, to her fury, her own singing voice was dubbed. She played a 'Hemingway woman' opposite Gregory Peck in *The Snows of Kilimanjaro*, 1952, in which both managed to act like mobile versions of Mount Rushmore. *Mogambo*, 1953, gave her a crack at Jean Harlow's old role in *Red Dust* and an Oscar nomination, as she entices Clark Gable away from a safe option. But it was Joseph Mankiewicz's *The Barefoot Contessa*, 1954, with Humphrey Bogart, that best summed up her personality as a fiery Spanish dancer who becomes a Hollywood legend. This, and her part in *Bhowani Junction*, 1956, as a half-caste Indian, were her best roles. Her salary continued to increase but her interest seemed to lapse, though she gave some credible performances in fairly mediocre movies during the late fifties, sixties and seventies; in *The Night of the Iguana*, 1964, she had exactly the sort of earthy, sleazy role she always liked best.

LEFT: studio portrait c. 1952.
    Photographer Virgil Apger

ROBERT MITCHUM

The recent, somewhat belated, enthusiasm for *Out of the Past*, 1947, has rightly elevated Robert Mitchum to his status as one of the great movie actors. It was his classic role; the warm, wisecracking private-eye Jeff Markham, who is trying to escape a past flame, 'Nothing mattered except I had her'. A natural performer whose strong and unsmilingly humorous presence has been compared with that of Bogart, he is more rugged and stoical, less moral and vulnerable. 'You look like you're in trouble,' says a taxi-driver to private-eye Mitchum, 'because you don't look like it,' and that sums up the appealing ambiguity of Mitchum's lizard-eyed insouciance and nonchalant toughness.

As an adolescent, Mitchum got into trouble with the authorities, fleeing from a week's service on a chain gang at the age of sixteen, and by the time he drifted into acting he had worked as a nightclub bouncer, ditch-digger, professional boxer and screenwriter. He started as a heavy in a series of Hopalong Cassidy Westerns, but his big break came in *The Story of G.I. Joe*, 1945, for which he was nominated for an Oscar as Best Supporting Actor. Other outstanding films include *Pursued*, 1947, *Angel Face*, 1952, *The Night of the Hunter*, 1955, *The Sundowners*, 1960, and *Two for the Seesaw*, 1962. Married for ages, despite some sizzling affairs, he has one daughter and two sons, both of whom have become actors.

ABOVE: *Macao*, 1952, with Jane Russell
LEFT: *Out of the Past*, 1947, with Virginia Huston
OPPOSITE: publicity portrait for *Where Danger Lives*, 1950

KIM NOVAK

As a young model Kim Novak played the part of 'Miss Deepfreeze', demonstrating refrigerators to eager purchasers. Was this just coincidence? The title is unerringly apt for this sad-eyed blonde with the icy smile, whom chance led to one of the greatest connoisseurs of the species, Alfred Hitchcock. Novak is the very core of his *Vertigo*, 1958, a swirling vortex of memory and obsession in which Novak's blandly anonymous features and hesitant air take on a mesmerizing force. The battle against her frozen inexpressiveness brings out a hitherto hidden warmth which engulfs her co-star James Stewart. Stewart's naturally gawky charm was the direct opposite of Novak's own appeal, and they teamed together again well in *Bell, Book and Candle*, also 1958.

This was her peak, when she displaced even Marilyn Monroe in the hearts of the American public; and it is tempting to say that her very blankness gave her the edge in popularity, for a short time at least. She had started out as Columbia's replacement for Rita Hayworth, and to many people's surprise the studio publicity campaign worked. She caught Sinatra's eye in *The Man With the Golden Arm*, and hit the big time opposite William Holden in *Picnic*, both 1955. Her screen charisma was low in *Pal Joey*, but she made up for it with the gutsy starring role as *Jeanne Eagels*, both 1957, a tinseltown booze-and-drugs biopic. She went through the motions of stardom and emerged on the giddy heights of *The Legend of Lylah Clare*, 1968, but in truth came over best opposite Dean Martin in Billy Wilder's satirical *Kiss Me, Stupid*, 1964, when even she seemed to be able to relax and take her star status more lightly.

RIGHT: *Jeanne Eagels*, 1957

MARLON BRANDO

Brando uses his body rather than his script, expressing emotion and sensuality with an extraordinary potency. Variously labelled during his early career as the Walking Hormone Factory, the Male Garbo, the Valentino of the Bop Generation and the Slob, he responded suitably by calling Hollywood 'a cultural boneyard'. Few other actors have inspired such polar reactions of critical rage and admiration, but there can be no argument that he is the most important actor of the modern cinema in America. He redrew the paradigms for leading men in the fifties and his influence can be traced to Jack Nicholson and Robert De Niro.

Brando's background was middleclass. His father was a prosperous manufacturer and his mother wrote, painted and was prominently involved in the local theatre. As a youngster, Brando was aggressive and rebellious – his spell in a military academy ending in expulsion, after which he took off for New York where he enrolled under Stella Adler in what was later to become the Actors' Studio. There he learned the Stanislavsky 'Method', a naturalistic approach to acting and character interpretation, and became the cinema's first notable exponent of the style (Brando starred in films several years before James Dean). It provided the foundations of his extraordinary technical skills, but was nevertheless the medium of, rather than the source for, his own disturbing presence as the brute male: bulky, crude and unwashed, he represents a primitive and uncompromising eroticism. But Brando is more than a big slob – his power and his threat lie in his frightening seriousness, and the sense of unreleased passion one can only just glimpse.

Brando became a star via Broadway, playing the crass, mumbling, violent Stanley Kowalski who rapes his nymphomaniac sister-in-law in Tennessee Williams's 'A Streetcar Named

RIGHT: studio portrait, 1950.
Photographer John Engstead

ABOVE: *A Streetcar Named Desire*, 1951, with Vivien Leigh

Desire'. Of the film offers which subsequently deluged him, he accepted the role of a paraplegic war veteran in *The Men*, 1950; Brando characteristically moved into a veterans' hospital to prepare for it, even insisting that a urine bottle be strapped to his leg. A year later, he recreated his stage role for the screen version of *Streetcar*, with Vivien Leigh. Even though the script was inevitably toned down by the Hays Office, the movie was magnificent and was hugely successful at the box office, making Brando a major screen star.

He went on to take some of the classic leading-men roles of the fifties. After *Viva Zapata!*, 1952, for which his make-up included the painful insertion

of plastic rings into his nostrils to flair them, and Antony in *Julius Caesar*, in 1953, he showed that the power of his presence and technical ability were more effective in contemporary drama: as ex-boxer Terry Malloy, 'I could have been a contender . . . instead of a bum', in the classic *On the Waterfront*, 1954, a Damon Runyon gambler in *Guys and Dolls*, 1955, and the motorbike rebel of *The Wild One* in 1953.

Brando's own love life was always stormy. He had short affairs with Shelley Winters and Eva Marie Saint, among others, and a more complicated one with France Nuyen; they had a son and she had a nervous breakdown. In *Reflections in a Golden*

Eye, 1967, he played an army officer, a repressed homosexual, patting his hair and smiling vainly as he lusts after private Robert Forster. Allegations of homosexuality never bothered him, 'Like a large number of men', he once said, 'I too have had homosexual experiences, and I'm not ashamed'. His first marriage to Anna Kashfi, in 1957, resulted in copious sordid revelations after the relationship fell apart in 1959; his second marriage, to Movita, a Mexican actress he met during the filming of *Viva Zapata!*, was also turbulent. More recently he set up home with a Tahitian girl, Tarita, in isolation

RIGHT: *On the Waterfront*, 1954, with
       Eva Marie Saint
BELOW: *The Wild One*, 1953, with Mary Murphy

on an island, and is fiercely protective of their privacy.

The sixties marked a fall in Brando's popularity. Most of his films either did badly financially, or did him little credit; he also fell out with Hollywood. In 1972, he triumphantly resuscitated his career with a superb piece of character acting in the role of Don Corleone in *The Godfather*, for which he won an Oscar; characteristically, caring little for Hollywood's ways, he asked an unknown American Indian actress to turn down the award on his behalf because of 'the treatment of American Indians in the motion picture industry'. Later, though, he was to give the finest per-

formance of his career in *Last Tango in Paris*, producing all the primitiveness and potency of his youth as he takes Maria Schneider to the depths of sexual humiliation. At the end, when Schneider shoots him, he takes the chewing-gum from his mouth and puts it neatly under some railings before he crumples to the floor, dead – a classic Brando moment.

ABOVE: publicity portrait for *Last Tango in Paris*, 1972

OPPOSITE: studio portrait, 1953.
Photographer Gene Korman

Now that her image is available on everything from pillowcases and hamburgers to posters and fine art, Marilyn Monroe may be said to have transcended her own time once and for all. She has entered the dizzy realm of twentieth-century myth as an American icon, a leading lady to the world, whose likeness has been novelized by Norman Mailer, painted by Andy Warhol, and impersonated by thousands of drag acts all over the world. Yet although her pouting lips, wiggling walk and platinum blonde hair are familiar to most who have not lived inside a vault for the last thirty years, in this context it is worth recalling just how *ordinary* her rise to fame was.

It was, after all, a traditional starlet's rise, after a famously unhappy childhood. Illegitimate, with a mentally ill mother, Norma Jean Mortenson lived in a series of foster homes and orphanages until she escaped, aged sixteen, by marriage. Her rise to fame began with model work, her brown hair now bleached and bobbed, and she made a slow start as an actress, suffering bit-parts, walk-ons and unrenewed contracts in five years of good and bad. She was pursued by Groucho Marx in *Love Happy*, 1949, patronized by George Sanders in *All About Eve*, 1950, and pacified by Richard Widmark in *Don't Bother to Knock*, 1952. Like a soft-centred, musical version of Harlow, she swept through leading roles in *Gentlemen Prefer Blondes* and *How to Marry a Millionaire*, both 1953, but still with elements of uncertainty visible amid the glamour and glitz of those productions. It was not until *The Seven Year Itch*, 1955, that she began to show the confidence expected of

the major star she had become. Yet, oddly for such a supposedly all-American sex symbol, her personification of fifties eroticism came over as that of a dream girl from another planet: breathy, cartoon-like, streamlined, pneumatic. She sensed the desire for unreality, and made it flesh.

Her ambition to be considered as an actress rather than a glamour queen was understandable and not untypical of that era's vogue for seriousness; but she did show real acting talent in *Bus Stop*, 1956, in which her brittle sexiness was taken over by a genuine tenderness and affection. The trouble was that whenever she was poured

ABOVE: publicity portrait for *The Seven Year Itch*, 1955.
Photographer Frank Powolny
OPPOSITE: studio portrait, c. 1952

into a satin dress and primed to wiggle and giggle, the old Monroe myth returned without any bidding; *Some Like it Hot*, 1959, became a superb farce as a result. Only *The Misfits*, 1961, among her last films shows a maturing actress destined for greatness, and she is immensely moving next to another Hollywood icon, in the shape of Clark Gable, who seems about to expire with every breath.

By this time Monroe's personal problems were interfering with her professional life. Frequently ill, under psychiatric care and subject to extreme nerves before the cameras, Monroe could be hostile and aggressive. Her colleagues' impatience got her dismissed from the set of her last film, *Something's Got to Give.*

Her sad death a month later incarnated her as an exhibit in the pop museum of Americana, along with Elvis and Coca-Cola. She had associated with the brawn (Joe DiMaggio), the brain (Arthur Miller) and even with the uncrowned royalty of America, the Kennedys, and her yearning after the great symbols of American life and hope through the medium of movies seems in retrospect almost conscious. When one begins to realize that, and then takes stock of her undoubted talents and wasted life, it perhaps seems that there was little ordinary about Marilyn Monroe after all.

ABOVE: publicity portrait for *How to Marry a Millionaire*, 1953
RIGHT: publicity portrait for *The Prince and the Showgirl*, 1957.
Photographer Richard Avedon

OPPOSITE: studio portrait, 1946.
Photographer A. L. 'Whitey' Schafer

Douglas's screen persona is that of the driven man: a self-centred, volcanic and relentless spirit reflected in extra-ordinarily cold, fierce eyes. That persona found perfect expression in his finest performance – the part of Dax, the First World War officer in Kubrick's *Paths of Glory*, 1957, who takes on the corrupt bureaucracy of the army in order to try and secure justice for a unit court-martialled for mutiny. In both *The Bad and the Beautiful*, 1952, and *Out of the Past*, 1947, he became a more unorthodox kind of hero – a supreme egotist who will do anything to get what he wants.

Although Douglas's image is that of the virile American, he was in fact the son of Russian immigrants and made it the hard way, putting himself through university and drama school by working as a waiter, a professional wrestler and a bell-hop. He made his Broadway debut in 1941, broke off to do war service in the navy, then made several films before hitting the jackpot in 1949 with *Champion*, playing a boxer who would K.O. his own granny to get to the top. In the fifties and sixties, he went on to make a string of exceptional films: apart from *Paths of Glory* his credits include *Ace in the Hole*, 1951, *Lust for Life*, 1956, *Spartacus*, 1960, and *Two Weeks in Another Town*, 1962.

ABOVE: publicity portrait for *The Big Sky*, 1952
LEFT: *The Bad and the Beautiful*, 1952, with Lana Turner

GRACE KELLY

Grace Kelly was always regarded as a valuable jewel: ice-cold, hard and glacial, sparkling, serene and timeless. She was regarded as Hollywood aristocracy even before proving herself as an actress, and her ascent to the fairy-tale heights of Princess Grace of Monaco was entirely in accordance with her personality and public image. She was somewhat too cool as Gary Cooper's wife in *High Noon*, 1952, and limpid opposite Gable and Ava Gardner in *Mogambo*, 1953, but she was the precise focus for Alfred Hitchcock's desires in an important trio of movies.

He once referred to his taste, where women were concerned, for 'the drawing-room type, the real ladies, who become whores once they're in the bedroom'. And, a voyeuristic glee in her fate notwithstanding, that is how he presents her in *Dial M for Murder*, 1954, where she is almost strangled; in *Rear Window*, 1954, in which she offers an invalided James Stewart a provocative come-on in her nightgown; and in *To Catch a Thief*, 1955, where she is decidedly upper-crust opposite Cary Grant. She is quite likeable in all these, with a sex appeal best likened to that of ice thawing; but she appears virtually oblivious to the sadistic innuendo implicit in the way she was being observed by her director. Amongst the dross in which she appeared before her famous marriage in 1956, her role in *High Society*, 1956, stands out. Her dove-like rendition of 'True Love' with Bing Crosby compensated for any static elegance in the former Katharine Hepburn role. It was actually a better performance than that in *The Country Girl*, 1954, also with Crosby, for which she won a Best Actress Oscar.

ABOVE: publicity portrait for *Rear Window*, 1954.
Photographer Bud Fraker
LEFT: publicity for *To Catch a Thief*, 1955, with Cary Grant

JAMES DEAN

A week after James Dean completed his seventh film, he catapulted himself into oblivion and popular myth in his new silver Porsche: he was only twenty-four. Like Valentino and Monroe, Dean had been crystallized in a particular time by his tragic and premature death, but in his case the effect was immeasurably sharpened by his youth and the fact that his legend as the spiritual leader of a generation rests, quite uniquely, on only two movies. In both of them, *East of Eden*, 1955, and *Rebel without a*

OPPOSITE: portrait, 1955.
　　　　　Photographer Sanford Roth
LEFT: portrait, c. 1954
BELOW: *Rebel without a Cause*, 1955, with Natalie Wood

Cause, 1955, he played restless, anguished heroes of burgeoning youth culture, embodying rebellion against middle-class values and hypocritical, suburban parents. As Jim in *Rebel*, he screams at his weak, indecisive, pinny-wearing father, 'I want answers now, I'm not interested in what I'll understand ten years from now'. Sulkily beautiful, he slunk around in jeans which were too tight, sneering and pouting and refusing to look adults in the eye, unloving and unlovable to them, because they either ignored him or substituted material goods for the understanding and loving acceptance he craved. His potency, though, was less in his youth than in the sadness and world-weariness he brought to his roles. Again, as Jim, when Buzz slashes his tyres, he drawls, 'You know something? You read too many comic books'. And then, when Buzz challenges Jim to a 'chicken run' and he agrees without knowing exactly what it is, except that it is dangerous, and asks his father if he should do something to save his honour, his father can tell him only not to rush into anything. The key to Dean's character was his rage and disenchantment against a world that has lost its nobility.

Dean's screen persona did not entirely have to be constructed. He had a sad, disrupted childhood himself; when he was five the family left their home in Indiana for Los Angeles, but three years later when his mother died his father sent him back to a farm in Indiana to be raised by relatives. After graduating from high school, he returned to California to attend college and began acting in a small theatre group. He made one or two television commercials, then landed bit parts in three films – *Sailor Beware*, *Fixed Bayonets* and *Has Anybody Seen My Gal* – all 1951 and 1952. Later that year he went to New York to work with the Actors' Studio and hung around the theatres, absorbing the influences that

LEFT: *East of Eden*, 1955

turned him, like Brando, into a new kind of flawed leading man with a new acting style. Eventually he landed parts in two Broadway plays, 'See the Jaguar' and 'The Immoralist', and won the screen test with Warner which took him to Hollywood.

Dean's third major film was *Giant*, 1956, in which he had to age fifty years from a youthful wanderer to a business tycoon. The week after shooting finished, 30 September 1955, Dean crashed his car; the impact almost severed his head from his body. Ironically, his voice had only recently been heard in a road safety campaign advert, warning 'Remember, the next life you save could be mine'.

Within only a few years the Dean mythology had produced numerous books and three movies: *The James Dean Story*, 1957, and *James Dean – The First American Teenager*, 1975, and, two years later, *September 30, 1955*. His style has not dated; thirty years from his death, Matt Dillon has arrived as 'the new James Dean'.

ABOVE: *Giant*, 1956, with Elizabeth Taylor

ELIZABETH TAYLOR

Unlike, say, Marilyn Monroe, whose whole existence seemed to resonate with the era of Eisenhower and of Kennedy's America, Elizabeth Taylor has never seemed representative of any special historical period or style. Instead she may be likened to a Hollywood star that has grown to incredible brightness but has found no sure direction, one that sucks bits of debris from other galaxies into its orbit. She is one of the last examples of that type of stardom. Her career has been erratic, wasteful and uncertain in all but ambition, and it is her private life – in particular her seven well-publicized marriages – that ousts her films as the main object of interest.

If she seems to have been with cinema audiences for a very long time, it is because of her childhood stardom that lasted from *Lassie Come Home*, 1943, and *National Velvet*, 1944, right up to her coming of age at eighteen as Spencer Tracy's daughter in *Father of the Bride*, 1950. Most of her best work falls within the next decade, and she changed films at only a slightly greater pace than her husbands: from Conrad Hilton Jr to Michael Wilding, from Mike Todd to Eddie Fisher, then from Richard Burton to Richard Burton and eventually to John Warner. Her romantic first in movies was Robert Taylor in *Conspirator*, 1949, but she proved better in roles that demanded more spirited histrionics. She was outstandingly desirable in *A Place in the Sun*, 1951, made a strong presence opposite James Dean in *Giant*, 1956, and was Oscar nominated for her performance opposite Montgomery Clift in *Raintree County*, 1957. She seemed to blossom in the face of Clift's neuroticism, for her own talent was for steamier, more bulldozing kinds of passion. She learnt how to exploit that style to maximum effect in adaptations of two Tennessee Williams plays, *Cat on a Hot Tin Roof*, 1958, with Paul

OPPOSITE: studio portrait, 1953.
        Photographer Bud Fraker
ABOVE: *Conspirator*, 1949, with Robert Taylor
LEFT: *A Place in the Sun*, 1951, with
   Montgomery Clift

Newman, and opposite Clift again for *Suddenly, Last Summer*, 1959; she emerged Oscar nominated for both performances and near the top of the box office attractions.

Nevertheless, her acting never got more than grudging reviews, and it was said that the Oscar she won for *Butterfield 8*, 1960, was awarded out of sympathy for a serious dose of pneumonia. She certainly gave a mediocre performance in that film, but afterwards seemed to take herself more seriously. *Cleopatra*, 1963, was the beginning of her romance with Burton but the end of her days of un-selfconscious glory as the queen of classy but likeable trash. Taylor and Burton together seemed to inspire each other to ever-increasing heights of embarrassment, plodding wearily through fiascos like *The Sandpiper*, 1965, and *The Comedians*, 1967. *Reflections in a Golden Eye*, 1967, was only saved by the substitution for Burton of Brando. Burton and Taylor were good value, however, in theatrical screaming matches like *Who's Afraid of Virginia Woolf?*, 1966, for which Taylor won an Oscar, and *The Taming of the Shrew*, 1967, which had a redeeming sense of humour.

In the final analysis Taylor has transcended her screen career to become a kind of *paparazzi* version of Helen of Troy. She has joined that select band of media figures like Monroe and Jackie Onassis whose souls have been sucked from them by the flash, bang and wallop of a million flashbulbs.

ABOVE: off set *The Girl Who Had Everything*, 1953
RIGHT: *Cat on a Hot Tin Roof*, 1958, with Paul Newman

Burton's popularity as a romantic figure peaked with his off-screen relationship with Elizabeth Taylor during the making of *Cleopatra*, 1963; they went on to marry and divorce twice in one of the flashiest, most public romances of the century. Of the films they made together only Mike Nichols's drama *Who's Afraid of Virginia Woolf?* drew from Burton the fire of which he was capable. *The Sandpiper*, 1965, and *The Taming of the Shrew*, 1967, were more romantic but equally hollow productions.

Burton was born into a huge family in a mining community in Wales and his rich, theatrical voice never completely lost its Welsh lilt. He won a scholarship to Oxford, built up a considerable reputation on the British stage, and attained Hollywood fame playing the romantic lead opposite Olivia de Havilland in *My Cousin Rachel*, 1953. His youthfully vibrant screen persona aged with him into the poignant image of a world-weary hero: contrast the fiery Burton who played Jimmy Porter in *Look Back In Anger* in 1959 with the disillusioned secret agent of the 1965 film *The Spy Who Came in from the Cold*, both starring roles opposite Claire Bloom. Drinking problems, illness and marital break-ups inevitably damaged his work, and during the seventies he fetched up in some rather undistinguished films. He died while filming *1984*, which had offered him his most interesting role for years.

RIGHT: studio portrait, c. 1959.
Photographer Bert Six

SIMONE SIGNORET

In *Casque d'or*, 1952, Simone Signoret looks as though she has descended from a Renoir painting, all lace and elaborate jewellery, sparkling eyes and a flashing smile. Yet by the time she made *Room at the Top*, only seven years later, she is already the 'older woman', her face resonant with experience, proudly passionate and serious about love. Signoret belonged to a generation of French actresses for whom age did not mean losing looks but gaining experience; and it was for the latter that she was valued. She won a Best Actress Oscar for her role as the discarded lover of Laurence Harvey, and rightly so. For even as a fresh, young girl in her twenties, she had managed to communicate a sense of pain and worldly knowledge at which most actresses – and actors – could only guess.

After bit-parts in Paris during the Second World War, she rose to prominence in Max Ophüls' splendid *La Ronde*, 1950, quickly followed by *Casque d'or* and a role as the adulteress in Marcel Carné's *Thérèse Raquin*, 1953. She always seemed to play a woman from whom pleasure was sought illicitly, but managed to select her parts as prostitutes and good-time girls with discrimination. As one of the plotters in *Les Diaboliques*, 1955, she was effortlessly convincing; but in later years, notably in *Ship of Fools*, 1965, her woman-of-the-world role became clichéd and overblown. She was always suited to an era of strong commitments and seemed out of step with modern complacency. Her famous marriage to Yves Montand (her first was to director Yves Allégret) brought with it a real-life role as the female half of France's most glamorous left-wing couple.

ABOVE: *Thérèse Raquin*, 1953, with Raf Vallone
OPPOSITE: *Casque d'or*, 1952, with
      Claude Dauphin
OVER: Paul Newman, publicity portrait

THE SIXTIES

WARREN BEATTY

Beatty's superstar persona is that of a charismatic, but ultimately helpless, male moved by forces beyond his control; it is that combination of rebellion and impotence, as well as his traditional good looks, which makes him so attractive. The image was first defined in *Bonnie and Clyde,* 1967, in which he played the wayward and impotent small-time crook, Clyde Barrow, whose semi-comic exploits with Faye Dunaway ended in bloody retribution from the establishment. In fact, having been impressed by the script, Beatty had hired the director, Arthur Penn, produced the film himself and forced the studio to redistribute it after initial box-office failure – an indication of his considerable entrepreneurial abilities which were to emerge more clearly over the next decade.

The younger brother of Shirley MacLaine, Beatty made his debut in Kazan's *Splendor in the Grass,* 1961, and found one of his most interesting early starring roles as the neurotic nightclub comic in *Mickey One,* his first film with Arthur Penn. After the success of *Bonnie and Clyde,* he co-scripted and produced *Shampoo,* 1975, playing the Beverly Hills super-stud hairdresser who beds his steady (Goldie Hawn) and his rival's wife, daughter and mistress (Julie Christie) in the course of the working day. The leading-man image suggested by the movie was enhanced by the fact he had yet to be pinned down in his private life.

Since then Beatty has produced, co-scripted and starred in two more major films. In the first, *Heaven Can Wait,* 1978, he played an American footballer who dies before schedule, and is sent back to earth to occupy the body of a tycoon in order to undo the character's anti-social business practices. The second, *Reds,* 1981, a big-screen political epic, traced the career of John Reed, a founder of the American Communist party, and featured a great on- and off-screen romance with Diane Keaton.

OPPOSITE: *All Fall Down,* 1962
ABOVE: *Bonnie and Clyde,* 1967, with Faye Dunaway

SEAN CONNERY

The James Bond spy thrillers made Sean Connery one of the biggest screen sex symbols in the world. Accessorized by small guns and a bevy of glamorous ladies, he lent Ian Fleming's smoothie spy the necessary wit and protective virility to make him hugely appealing as a fantasy lover and hero for the sixties. Debonair in a rugged Scottish way, he was extraordinarily sexy, upper class but cosmopolitan and able to take on all comers.

The first Bond movie, the enormously successful *Dr No*, 1962, was followed by *From Russia with Love*, 1963, *Goldfinger*, 1964, and *Thunderball*, 1965. Connery was already trying to break away from the image, as the forceful Mark Rutland in *Marnie*, 1964, and as the obsessively rebellious prisoner in *The Hill*, 1965. However, he has found it difficult to leave Bond behind and exploit his quality of glossy butchiness in more intelligent films, in part because his fans have not wanted him to: neither Roger Moore nor George Lazenby have lived up to his success in the role. He made two more Bond movies, *You Only Live Twice*, 1967, and *Diamonds Are Forever*, 1971, then took on a variety of new roles, notably *The Anderson Tapes*, 1971, and *The Man Who Would Be King*, 1975. But the suave spy continued to dog him – he returned to the screen as Bond in *Never Say Never Again*, a reworking of *Thunderball*, made outside the control of Bond movie creator and producer 'Cubby' Broccoli.

LEFT: *From Russia with Love*, 1963

OPPOSITE: *Bonnie and Clyde*, 1967

Just when you thought there could never be another Joan Crawford . . . along comes Faye Dunaway. Her hysterically camp portrayal of a real-life Crawford in *Mommie Dearest*, 1981, seemed at first sight to be a calculated piece of Grand Guignol, a berserk overstatement of a larger-than-life character. But looking back you can't be so sure. For Dunaway's sense of melodrama, and of herself as the *grand dame* of the genre, may well have been nurturing itself over the years.

She didn't start out that way. For years after her Oscar-nominated performance with Warren Beatty in *Bonnie and Clyde*, 1967, she remained Bonnie Parker, the cigar-chewing, machine-gun toting Southern gal transformed into a soft-focus romantic out-

law. From there she drifted into *The Thomas Crown Affair*, 1968, a caper movie with Steve McQueen, and on into the adult entanglements of Elia Kazan's *The Arrangement*, 1969; but neither dispelled the rosy hue of *Bonnie*. It was not until Roman Polanski came along with *Chinatown*, 1974, that she found a part she could get her teeth into.

And how. . . . As Mrs Evelyn Mulwray, Dunaway was the poisonous heart of a plot which skids from *film noir* into the deep waters of family melodrama without the audience guessing. She starts as the object of detective Jack Nicholson's investigation, but ends by stealing his movie with a performance of intense emotional power, one which hints at Craw-

ford's eye-rolling frenzy and leaves the audience devastated.

Network, 1976, gave her both an Oscar and all the opportunities she needed to indulge in angry histrionics; after that Dunaway had to wait until *Mommie Dearest* to provide another true she-monster for her. Her interpretation of the *The Wicked Lady*, 1983, did not suggest that Dunaway wanted to change, but the time may yet come when she does.

ABOVE: *The Thomas Crown Affair*, 1968, with Steve McQueen

Paul Newman has come to represent, in both his films and his private life, the 'good' outsider; detached, ironic and idealistic despite his iconoclastic streak. It was a unique combination of desirable male qualities that made him one of the biggest male stars of the sixties and seventies. Even now, at the age of sixty, his bravado, strength and stunningly good looks are still admired by women, men and critics; his amused half smile and famous blue eyes still convey a youthful irreverence as well as a very appealing trace of self-detraction.

Although Newman's career started in the late fifties, his biggest popular success came in 1969 with the male buddy film *Butch Cassidy and the Sundance Kid*, in which the true tale of two Western outlaws became that of a pair of lovable pranksters whose friendship ends in instant and mutual oblivion. As in *The Sting*, 1973, for which Newman and Redford were teamed up again by George Roy Hill, this time as engaging con-men, the movie tapped a very strong but usually unarticulated source of male emotion – the brusquely unromantic but loyal commitment to a fellow male that is usually suppressed after schooldays. Intriguingly, Newman and Redford were never close friends themselves, and both have strongly uxorial private lives: Newman's marriage to actress Joanne Woodward has been one of the most durable in Hollywood.

Newman was born into an affluent background; his Jewish father owned a sports goods store, and his mother was a Catholic who became a devout Christian Scientist and tried to bring her son up in the faith. Newman performed plays in high school, majored in economics at college, was a radio-man on torpedo bombers in the Second World War, considered becoming a teacher and then, on the death of his father, took over the family business. Very swiftly realizing that the sports

RIGHT: publicity portrait for *The Long, Hot Summer*, 1958

goods industry was not for him, he handed over to his brother and, after drama school, ended up in New York at Lee Strasberg's Actors' Studio.

His first screen roles were very much in the Brando mould – neurotic, mirthless, mumbling and bolshy. Like him, he played Tennessee Williams's anti-heroes, in *Cat on a Hot Tin Roof*, 1958, and *Sweet Bird of Youth*, 1962, for which he received the first of his Oscar nominations; at one stage he was even labelled the New Brando. Within a few years, though, a new and more distinctive character was emerging – a male whose macho demeanour and tongue-in-cheek bravado concealed sexual fears and social inadequacy. In *The Hustler*, 1961, *Hud*, 1963, and *Cool Hand Luke*, 1967, he displayed a mixture of strength, devilment and vulnerability with which many men could identify. These 'loner' films gave way to the individualist heroes of the early to mid-seventies, notably in *The Life and Times of Judge Roy Bean*, 1972, and *Buffalo Bill and the Indians*, 1976. Newman's sexual attractiveness continued into middle-age despite, or perhaps because of, his honesty in playing characters vulnerable to the disillusioning and depleting forces of time. One of his outstanding performances of the seventies was in *Slap Shot*, 1977, playing a battered, foul-mouthed coach of a washed-up ice hockey team. Far from gliding into distinguished seniority as an aging sex-symbol, Newman also relished the opportunity to present himself as unglamorously as possible as an alcoholic failed lawyer in *The Verdict*, 1981.

In certain ways, Newman's private life conforms to the image of a Hollywood star; one of his great interests is racing cars, which he drives to a very high standard with several wins to his credit. But in other ways he remains an outsider. He is embarrassed by all the

ABOVE: *From the Terrace*, 1960, with Joanne Woodward
LEFT: *Cat on a Hot Tin Roof*, 1958, with Elizabeth Taylor

ABOVE: *Butch Cassidy and the Sundance Kid,*
1969, with Robert Redford

adulation that still comes his way, and is said to regard being asked to remove his dark glasses in the same way most women feel about being asked to expose their breasts. A vociferous liberal who actively participated in the Civil Rights movement and campaigns for the Democrats and gay rights, he often expresses boredom with acting. Newman has two daughters from his first marriage to Jacqueline Witter — their son Scott, a drama student, died in 1978 of a drug and alcohol overdose — and three daughters from his second marriage. He has acted with, or directed, wife Joanne Woodward in a string of films, from *Rachel Rachel*, 1968, and *Winning*, 1969, to *Harry and Son*, 1984, which have always been interesting and sometimes very good.

BRIGITTE BARDOT

Brigitte Bardot was the Lolita who conquered the world, a pouting teenager, half-child and half-woman, whose very initials came to stand for a sexual myth: 'la bébé'. She was a uniquely French creation, able to mix a talent for scandal with a knowing *naïveté*, and under the careful eyes of her first husband and lifelong friend Roger Vadim, she was guided towards international stardom as the incarnation of sexual freedom. She had graduated from secondary parts to leads by 1955, but Vadim's first film as director, *Et Dieu créa la femme . . ., 1956,* launched her throughout the world, netting $4,000,000 in box office receipts on the way. She became a public figure, a bikini-clad *Liberté* arousing drowsy French men and women to frolic in the waters of St Tropez like oversexed children. B.B. was an instant cult, fuelled by the photographs of the *paparazzi* who pursued her, and by scenes like her shameless seduction of Jean Gabin in *En cas de malheur*, 1958. The basis of her appeal was not her acting but rather a protracted promise of striptease, that never failed to titillate her public even as far on as *Viva Maria*, 1965. She had little of that saving distance that a Dietrich might seek to retain. Her effect was blinding, dazzling, exciting, like that of her true medium, publicity; but unlike that medium, Bardot has worn well and can still corner headlines in the international press. As an actress, only in Jean-Luc Godard's *Le Mépris/ Contempt*, 1963, was she used with intelligence, and she gave perhaps her best performance as a movie star dazed at the confusion between her real life and the fake world of the movies, of which her bleached blonde hair was the constant reminder.

OPPOSITE: studio portrait, 1957
ABOVE: publicity portrait for *Doctor at Sea*, 1955
LEFT: *Et Dieu créa la femme . . .*, 1956, with
    Jean-Louis Trintignant

197

JEAN-PAUL BELMONDO

Belmondo rose to overnight fame as the Bogart-worshipping anti-hero of *Breathless*, 1960, and, with a notable performance as the slightly deranged hero of *Pierrot Le Fou*, 1965, established himself as an existentialist figurehead to the rebellious youth of the sixties with a persona that contained elements of James Dean, Humphrey Bogart, and even Marlon Brando.

Simultaneously abrasive, sensitive, anti-social and tender, his outlaw image is less chillingly psychopathic than that of Alain Delon, with whom he revelled in new excesses of criminality in *Borsalino*, 1970; his dog-eared features and hurt, resigned eyes contrast engagingly with Delon's icy prettiness. The son of a sculptor, he went on to take over from Jean Gabin as France's most popular screen star, an actor of great virtuosity who has played roles ranging from louts to students to factory workers, priests and even a French Robin Hood in *Cartouche*, 1962. Nowadays he tends to stick to playing his gangster persona in commercial, lighthearted thrillers, and his notable appearances in the seventies included the swindling protagonist of *Stavisky*, 1974, in which he invested money; he now heads his own production company.

RIGHT: publicity portrait for *Moderato Cantabile*, 1960

Barbra Streisand is above all a performer. She possesses a near-perfect instinct for knockout showbiz schmaltz — but with a tendency to deliver a powerhouse punch where a more skilful cinema actress might achieve more with less. She started out as a singer with a driving ambition to act, and made her name on Broadway in 1962. Her first movie was as the kooky ugly duckling Fanny Brice in *Funny Girl*, 1968, an enormously successful movie that established this gawky twenty-six-year old as a serious superstar with an Oscar under her belt and a contract with CBS that would produce a clutch of million-selling records. Nevertheless her follow-up in *Hello, Dolly!*, 1969, was not successful, and *On a Clear Day You Can See Forever*, 1970, with Yves Montand, met a similar fate. *The Owl and the Pussycat*, 1970, and the Peter Bogdanovich comedy *What's Up Doc?*, 1972, showed a nascent talent for screwball craziness; *The Way We Were*, 1973, proved how sensitive she could get with Robert Redford, but *A Star Is Born*, 1976, and *The Main Event*, 1979, proved ear-thumping, eye-straining exercises in megalomania, although commercial successes for all that. Her ambitions triumphed when she wrote, directed, produced and starred in *Yentl*, 1983, but her crass sentimentalization of Isaac Bashevis Singer's story was ultimately unappealing, little more than a tearful wallow. Now only in her mid-forties (and divorced from Elliott Gould), she is a sort of Sarah Bernhardt of Hollywood, demanding attention for her own charisma with all the cultivated arrogance of a pop Brooklyn diva. No matter how multi-talented, she seems increasingly remote from contemporary concerns, as if show business provides all her questions and all her answers; and she fails to win fans among audiences who don't relish being yelled at in the stalls.

RIGHT: *Funny Girl*, 1968

JANE FONDA

There have been at least four Jane Fondas. There was a timid starlet in *The Chapman Report*, 1962, who grew into the space-fantasy sex-kitten of *Barbarella*, 1968; then the pro-Vietcong outspoken media figure of *Tout va bien*, 1972, was supplanted by the confident Hollywood actress. Since her Oscar nomination for *They Shoot Horses Don't They?*, 1969, and her Best Actress award for *Klute*, 1971, right up to *The China Syndrome*, 1979, .and *Nine to Five*, 1980, Fonda has reassured doubters – including herself – that there is still a chance to express modern feminist attitudes in a hidebound, male-dominated industry. Personally she has had a major triumph. The daughter of Henry Fonda, one-time wife of Roger Vadim, and well-known anti-establishment figure, she has managed to hijack the leadership of Hollywood's grand tradition of leading ladies and drag it into modern times. She fought for adult and mature roles concerning sensitive social issues in movies like *Julia*, 1977, *Coming Home*, 1978, *The Electric Horseman*, 1979, and *The China Syndrome*. And she has earned in her own right a widespread popularity all the more surprising after her public vilification in the sixties and seventies. But she can show her Hollywood weaknesses as well as her strengths. She is earnest but corny, comic but sentimental, passionate yet superficial; she can make an audience curl up in embarrassment moments after making them yell out hurrahs. *On Golden Pond*, 1981, allowed her an on-screen reconciliation with both her father and with the old Hollywood tradition in which she is rooted. She is the grandest 'inside outsider' of the film business, and has had to fight out her rebellion in the uncomfortable glare of the public; that alone has given her a perversely unique status.

LEFT: publicity portrait for *Cat Ballou*, 1965
OPPOSITE ABOVE: *Walk On the Wild Side*, 1962, with Laurence Harvey
OPPOSITE BELOW: *Julia*, 1977

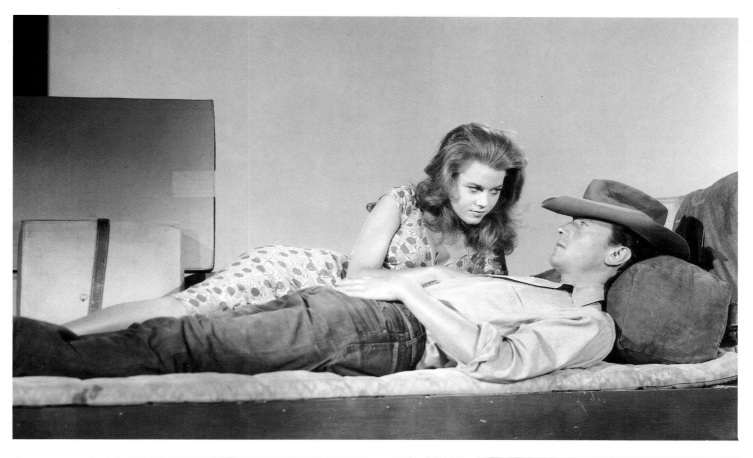

STEVE McQUEEN

A toughie with an affinity for hardware – guns, motorbikes, sports cars and handcuffs – Steve McQueen's leading men were stoical, cool and insolent loners, like the hero of *Bullitt*, the movie with the car chase to end all car chases, in which his persistent cop wins through as a human extension of a big, powerful, pulsating engine. Much seems to have been based on McQueen's own off-screen taste for racing cars and bikes.

Brought up by his grandparents, he was a troublesome adolescent who spent three years in a California reformatory, ran away from home and became a drifter, working on ships, as an oil-field labourer and as a fairground barker. Of his three-year stint with the navy he spent forty-one days in detention, suggesting that it was just as well he discovered he could act and found a place at drama school. He once said of himself, 'There's something about my shaggy-dog eyes that makes people think I'm good, but I'm really not all that good. I'm pretty much myself most of the time in my movies, and I've accepted that'. Like James Coburn, McQueen first shone in *The Magnificent Seven*, 1960, then went on to play the taciturn loner in *Hell is for Heroes*, 1962, and the heroic motorcycle freak of *The Great Escape*, 1963, who is captured bloodily entangled with his machinery in the barbed wire, and returned to the P.O.W. camp 'cooler'.

His heroes were often made unconventional by sensitivity and self-doubt, characteristics which extended his appeal to women as well as men. Of his roles in the sixties, the most interesting were the professional gambler in *The Cincinnati Kid*, 1965, the half-Indian cowboy tracking down his parents' killers in *Nevada Smith*, 1966, and as the ship's engineer attracted to Candice Bergen in *The Sand Pebbles*, 1966. In 1968 he abandoned his macho image for that of a more traditional romantic leading man in *The Thomas Crown Affair*, opposite Faye

LEFT: *The Great Escape*, 1963

Dunaway, in which he took the part of a seemingly respectable businessman who turns out to be in the business of robbing banks. It was his silliest movie, but by then he was a superstar.

In *Junior Bonner*, 1972, he reverted to his established persona to play an aging rodeo star and the same year, in *The Getaway*, he got mixed up with bank robbery, and with Ali MacGraw, who later became his second wife. *Papillon*, 1973, produced another characteristically tough, resilient performance as the real-life convict who battles to escape from cruelty and squalor on Devil's Island. He completed his last film, *Tom Horn*, 1980, while undergoing treatment for cancer; his third wife, Barbara Minty, was with him when he died the same year, following surgery, aged fifty.

RIGHT: publicity portrait for *Bullitt*, 1968
BELOW: *Love with the Proper Stranger*, 1963, with Natalie Wood

JULIE CHRISTIE

From the moment Julie Christie appeared as Tom Courtenay's dream girl in *Billy Liar*, 1963, she was seized on as the very epitome of the swinging sixties. Pushed through the acerbic fashion world of *Darling*, 1965, she emerged with an Oscar, as many American fans as the Beatles, and the successful contender for the Scarlett O'Hara role of the decade as Lara in *Doctor Zhivago*, 1965. She was beautiful without make-up, vivacious yet vulnerable, but had such an unaffected air it suggested her whole rise to fame was as much a surprise to her as to anybody else. She was deemed to have 'It', and thus defined the sixties as neatly as Clara Bow had symbolized the flappers of the twenties — yet she seemed to long to be 'without it'. She veered towards the arty side of commercial cinema for François Truffaut in *Fahrenheit 451*, 1966, and in *Far From the Madding Crowd*, 1967; and she was very much on form for the then off-form directors Joseph Losey and Robert Altman, in *The Go-Between* and *McCabe and Mrs Miller*, both 1971. (She was nominated for an Oscar for the latter.) *Don't Look Now*, 1973, caught her in the unfamiliar world of an erotically chilling thriller. By the time of *Shampoo*, 1975, and *Heaven Can Wait*, 1978, she had graduated to the Californian 'me'-centred world of Warren Beatty and seemed to be wondering whether these painstakingly light comedies were worth all the effort. Her answer was to turn down subsequent Hollywood offers in favour of roles that touched her conscience and her politics, such as the leads in *Memoirs of a Survivor*, 1981, *The Return of the Soldier*, 1982, and *Heat and Dust*, 1983, from novels by Doris Lessing, Rebecca West and Ruth Prawer Jhabvala respectively. More so than her American counterpart Jane Fonda, she seems to have decided that the movies hold little satisfaction for her.

LEFT: *Darling*, 1965

Michael Caine is an odd mixture of working-class charm and aristocratic arrogance, qualities which belie the ordinariness of his looks and which were at their most potent in *Alfie*, 1966, in which he chatted numerous females into bed and trouble without a hint of chivalry or remorse. The appeal of his mild-mannered toughness had been made clear by *The Ipcress File*, 1965, as the seedily heroic, bespectacled spy Harry Palmer, a leading man almost despite himself; a complete contrast to those two glossy British heroes, Sean Connery and Roger Moore, but it had taken the sexier image to make the appeal stick.

Born Maurice Micklewhite, in London, Caine had worked in the repertory theatre and for television and – rather ironically, given his later image – had his first big success as an aristocratic officer in *Zulu*, 1964. In the late sixties he went on to make several war films and thrillers, the best of which were *Gambit*, 1966, opposite Shirley Mac-Laine, and *The Italian Job*, 1969, a lovely caper/crime movie in which Caine played a small-time spiv running a big continental bullion robbery.

Caine underwent a re-evaluation in the seventies taking more serious roles in such films as *Sleuth*, 1972, and *The Man Who Would Be King* and in *The Romantic Englishwoman*, both 1975, in the latter playing a writer of fantasy fiction married to the discontented Glenda Jackson. Now in his fifties, he has retained his aura of appealing self-mockery, and in 1983 he was wonderful as the oddly romantic, academic drunk who falls for Julie Walters in *Educating Rita*.

RIGHT: publicity portrait for *Deadfall*, 1968

CATHERINE DENEUVE

Even if she was born twenty years too late to cultivate it, Catherine Deneuve was the very embodiment of the Hitchcockian ice-cold blonde, and a potentially more rewarding model than Kim Novak, Tippi Hedren or even Grace Kelly. Her role for Roman Polanski as the ill-fated heroine of *Repulsion*, 1965, showed that someone had indeed noticed her peculiarly frigid quality and her capacity for a razor's edge display of terror. It was an unlikely advance, however, for an actress who had started a career under the influence of Roger Vadim, and then made her name in Jacques Demy's colourful musical *Les Parapluies de Cherbourg*, 1964. She followed that success with a starring role, with her sister Françoise Dorléac, in Demy's *Les Demoiselles de Rochefort*, 1967; and in the same year she made Luis Buñuel's *Belle de Jour*. As the elegant Parisian housewife whose sexual fantasies lead her into part-time prostitution, Deneuve gave a definitive portrayal of a character whose calm surface belies seething depths of unpredictable passions. Her performance in Buñuel's *Tristana*, 1970, was similarly gripping, managing to create an atmosphere of stifling repression and crippled beauty; but although her roles persistently gained in stature during the seventies, and she became France's undisputed leading star, Truffaut's *Le Dernier Métro*, 1980, was a rare exploitation of her real abilities. Today she is thought of like some expensive perfume, but her image seems to contradict and trivialize her capacity as an actress. For despite two resolutely modern roles in *Repulsion* and *Belle de Jour*, and despite having consorted with such symbols of sixties modernity as Vadim, Marcello Mastroianni and photographer David Bailey, she remains an essentially conservative figure, orthodox and undissenting.

OPPOSITE: *Belle de Jour*, 1967, with Jean Sorel
RIGHT: *The Hunger*, 1983

OVER: Robert Redford, publicity portrait for *The Sting*, 1973.

MODERN TIMES

CLINT EASTWOOD

A quiet, self-reliant pussycat, tough with men but tender with chosen women, Clint Eastwood has a lazy, low-profile sexiness and a tantalizingly disciplined tension. Occasionally it metamorphoses into orgiastic viciousness. Although Eastwood is not as rugged as John Wayne, and his persona is neither straightforwardly paternalistic nor law-abiding, he nonetheless became one of America's ideal macho males in the seventies, and he is now usually regarded as the natural successor to Wayne's position as the foremost action film hero. At times, however, as in *Dirty Harry*, when Eastwood tortures a confession out of the killer he has hunted down, the persona is far more anti-heroic.

Much of that solitary persona ties in with Eastwood's own experience; born in San Francisco during the Depression years, he had an itinerant family life while his father travelled to find work. He was a self-sufficient, rather withdrawn boy whose only success at school was athletic. Later, he odd-jobbed as a truck driver and a lumberjack and coached swimming in the army. He drifted into movies through bit-parts and got his break in the television series *Rawhide*, in which he played the boyish, laid-back cowboy Rowdy Yates for seven years.

He first developed the figure of the cynical, idealistic wanderer dishing out revenge in a meaningless universe, as the 'Man with No Name' in Sergio Leone's trilogy of spaghetti Westerns, *A Fistful of Dollars*, 1964, *For a Few Dollars More*, 1965, and *The Good, the Bad and the Ugly*, 1966. The character was quite new – Eastwood recalls that he made it 'much more economical and much less expository' than the way it had originally been written – and was rapturously received. He then transferred the moral law-breaker to a modern, urban context as the cop who

OPPOSITE: *Dirty Harry*, 1971
ABOVE: *Play Misty for Me*, 1971, with
    Jessica Walter
LEFT: *Every Which Way But Loose*, 1978, with
    Sondra Locke

211

is not always prepared to go through the bureaucratic channels. In *Coogan's Bluff*, 1968, he played a deputy sheriff from Arizona who goes to New York to bring back a killer, and in *Dirty Harry*, 1971, a cop battling against red tape as he tracks down a sadistic murderer in San Francisco. Explaining the subtlety of his character's relationship with the law, Eastwood once said, 'There is a fantasy figure in this era of bureaucracy, of complicated life, income tax and politicizing everything, that there's a guy who can do certain things by himself. There'll always be that fantasy. I think there's an admiration for it'.

The same year, Eastwood directed and starred in the much under-rated *Play Misty for Me*, taking the role of a

disc-jockey unwillingly involved with a homicidal girl fan. Still a loner, the character presented himself more overtly as an emotional/sexual being, aware of a conflict between isolation and intimacy. Again, aspects of the character seemed close to Eastwood himself, a loner who avoids intrusion into his private life. This is also true of his relationships with women; he professes to be deeply in favour of monogamy, and his own marriage, to Maggie Johnson, lasted twenty-eight years.

One of the few superstars around, Eastwood has persevered with directing, accruing most critical acclaim for the epic Western *The Outlaw Josey Wales*, 1976. Eastwood abandoned serious drama to make the comic box-

office hit *Every Which Way But Loose*, 1978, starring alongside a gorilla and his real-life companion Sondra Locke, but in *Tightrope* he returned to a darker version of Dirty Harry, as a cop, Wes Block, tracking down a sex killer while himself subject to the same contorted, violent urges that drive his prey.

ABOVE: publicity portrait for *For a Few Dollars More*, 1965

OPPOSITE: publicity potrait for *Kramer vs Kramer*, 1979

Meryl Streep is a class act. She may not always be likeable. She may sometimes appear obsessively worthy, irritating, precious or theatrical. But it cannot be said she comes second on many lists of the best film actresses around. The worst that could be said is she seems to have too much taste for her own good. In a mere eight years since her first appearance in *Julia*, 1977, she has scarcely made a wrong move and has hogged the strongest parts around, from *Kramer vs Kramer*, 1979, to *The French Lieutenant's Woman*, 1981, *Sophie's Choice*, 1982, and *Silkwood*, 1983 — picking up a clutch of Oscars on the way. More

RIGHT: *Sophie's Choice*, 1982, with Kevin Kline
BELOW: *The French Lieutenant's Woman*, 1981, with Jeremy Irons

than that, she has carved out for herself a recognizable territory as a woman struggling with the problems of independence, which has confined her position as a resolutely contemporary actress.

Much of this was obvious even from a 'man's movie' like *The Deer Hunter*, 1978, in which Streep plays the girlfriend back home. She entered politics as a calculating and ambitious assistant to a senator in *The Seduction of Joe Tynan*, 1979, but that self-centred ruthlessness was tempered by a more sympathetic role as the divorcée in *Kramer vs Kramer*, in which she successfully stood up to Dustin Hoffman's practised scene-stealing techniques with credit.

Kramer's status as the archetypal modern weepie, one which cunningly shifts time-honoured plotting tech-

niques on to the scattered relationships of the 1970s, also emphasized Streep's tendency to tears. It never takes much to make Streep weep, and she has indeed opted for melodrama with an almost masochistic passion. *The French Lieutenant's Woman* is an example, a somewhat broken-backed affair dipping unsatisfactorily between ancient and modern settings. Streep's taste for trauma led her to the television soap opera 'Holocaust', 1978, and to *Sophie's Choice*, and in award-winning performances she took on the suffering of the Jews under Nazism with tear-stained virtuosity. *Plenty*, 1985, offered her a solo turn in another English guise as a woman on the edge of a nervous breakdown.

Streep comes from a middle-class, New Jersey Dutch background, and studied at Yale's famous drama

school; forty plays over three years trained and sharpened her technique, and that classical, theatrical grounding is worn on her sleeve as evidence of her good taste and pedigree dramatic breeding. But Streep's cool crisp precision is something less sympathetic than, for example, Ingrid Bergman's warmth and generosity, and perhaps her least traumatic venture *Falling in Love*, 1984, opposite Robert De Niro was a recognition of this, and an attempt to remedy it. It didn't. But for the time being at least, Streep's name will continue to feature in the lists of Oscar nominations (in 1986 for *Out of Africa*), and everyone else will continue to play second fiddle.

ABOVE: *Plenty*, 1985

ROBERT DE NIRO

De Niro's predatory and sometimes overpowering masculinity frightens and compels so effectively because in it can be sensed the barely submerged rage and violence of a trapped man. As Travis Bickle, the deranged urban avenger in *Taxi Driver*, 1976, and as the metal-worker in *The Deer Hunter*, 1978, trying to come to terms with his terrible experiences in Vietnam, he was immediately identifiable with the victims of the age. An actor of huge range and extraordinary sexual magnetism, with the power to create in a film the sense of the hellish world in which his character exists, his characters seem emotionally behind their time, incapable of confronting their female side. In *New York, New York*, 1977, his dominating, self-centred chauvinist tells Liza Minnelli, 'You don't say goodbye to me, I say goodbye to you'.

But, for all their macho posturing, De Niro's males often end up as romantic losers; in *New York, New York*, Minnelli frees herself from his dominance to become a star and bring up their son alone, and in *The Last Tycoon*, 1976, De Niro's elegant studio boss, modelled on Irving Thalberg, was caught up in a hopeless, illusory love affair. Whether as the demented Johnny Boy of *Mean Streets*, 1973, the coolly graceful Vito Corleone of *The Godfather, Part II*, 1974, or the primitive Jake La Motta in *Raging Bull*, 1980, De Niro appears to live his roles, even changing physically. 'I can't cheat when I act,' he said, 'I know that the cinema is an illusion, but not for me.'

LEFT: publicity portrait for *The Deer Hunter*, 1978

Jack Nicholson paid his acting dues with years of work on quickie exploitation movies. He was thirty years old when, as the drop-out lawyer in *Easy Rider*, 1969, he first grabbed the moviegoing public by the throat. It is not easy to upstage Nicholson, and he is so enjoyable to watch that no audience in its right mind would *want* him upstaged. He can easily romp away with the entire show, as he did with his over-the-top axe-wielding performance in *The Shining*, 1980, and with his pony-tailed devil fulminating about women in the *Witches of Eastwick*, 1987. He has also been known to steal the show with a cameo role, which he did playing Eugene O'Neill in *Reds*, 1981, and Shirley MacLaine's astronaut neighbour in *Terms of Endearment*, 1983. He was the bewildered centre-piece in *Chinatown*, 1974, playing the private eye who finds himself swamped by the complexities of a seemingly simple case, and he was both crazed and compassionate as McMurphy in *One Flew Over the Cuckoo's Nest*, 1975 (for which he won his first Oscar). His performance as the alcoholic down-and-out in *Ironweed*, 1978, showed up that of co-star Meryl Streep as mannered and artificial.

Nicholson is at home with drama, helping Jessica Lange to murder her husband in *The Postman Always Rings Twice*, 1981, and with comedy, as the dumb Mafia hitman in *Prizzi's Honor*, 1985, wondering whether to kill or to marry Kathleen Turner. And only Nicholson could bring the necessary combination of flamboyance and menace to the role of the joker in *Batman*, 1989. The track record is impressive, but the career is far from over: there are undoubtedly a lot of tricks left up his sleeve.

ABOVE: *The Postman Always Rings Twice*, 1981

ROSANNA ARQUETTE   MICHELLE PFEIFFER

When Rosanna Arquette was growing up as a child of the sixties she had pictures of Marilyn Monroe on her wall, but secretly wanted to be Natalie Wood. If Monroe was like an impossible dream, Wood's doe-eyed charm was something to aim for. Arquette showed tender toughness as Gary Gilmore's girlfriend in *The Executioner's Song*, 1982, and in *Baby, It's You*, 1983, and played the scatty housewife who is *Desperately Seeking Susan*, 1985. Arquette has a manic energy that earned her a role in Martin Scorsese's black comedy, *After Hours*, 1985, while her soulful expression was turned on for *Silverado*, 1985; suggesting that children of the eighties may one day want to grow up to be Rosanna Arquette.

BELOW: *The Executioner's Song*, 1982

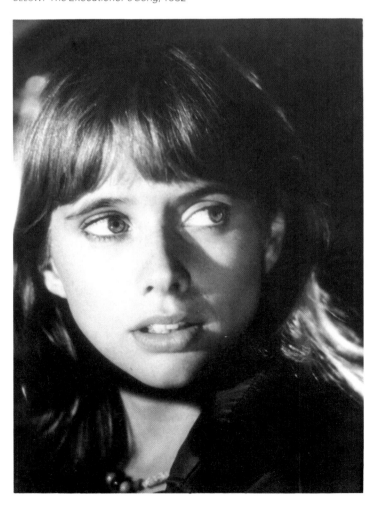

Michelle Pfeiffer was sufficiently eye-catching in *Scarface*, 1983, as Al Pacino's moll, and sufficiently kooky opposite Jeff Goldblum in *Into the Night*, 1985, for all the old comparisons to be wheeled out. She was as cheeky as Harlow, as crazy as Lombard, as vivacious as Monroe or as icy as Grace Kelly, depending on who might be your favourite. Pfeiffer has that blank stare of the made-to-measure Californian blonde which suggests she lives as much in the present tense as do her audiences. Certainly she looked out of place in the medieval *Ladyhawke*, 1985, and even in the fifties revival, *Grease II*, only really seeming at home in the laid-back Los Angeles night-time. Cool, cute and suntanned, she's the embodiment of 'California über alles'.

ABOVE: *Ladyhawke*, 1985

SIGOURNEY WEAVER   ISABELLE HUPPERT

As the meek and malleable heroine of *La Dentellière/The Lacemaker*, 1977, Isabelle Huppert's debut on the international scene was almost apologetic. Her own docile, freckled face seemed to capture so closely the character's restrained and tragic mood that she barely appeared to be acting; only with her role as the spiteful and bitter anti-heroine *Violette Nozière*, 1978, for Claude Chabrol was her range as an actress evident. Her selection for the Michael Cimino epic and spectacular flop *Heaven's Gate*, 1980, was a mixed blessing for her, and it was no surprise that she should return to France for *Sauve qui peut (la vie)/Slow Motion*, 1980, for Jean-Luc Godard. *Coup de torchon/Clean Slate* and *Passion*, both 1982, confirmed her as a bankable European star with little need for whatever Hollywood has to offer.

BELOW: portrait, 1980

Sigourney Weaver has it all: a first name plucked from 'The Great Gatsby', an M.A. from Yale Drama School, and those taut, chiselled looks so reminiscent of the Katharine Hepburn—Jane Fonda style. But she has yet to find the right leading role. She sparkled briefly with Mel Gibson in *The Year of Living Dangerously*, 1982, but her other male foils have ranged between a berserk New York spook in *Ghostbusters*, 1984, to a voyeuristic janitor in *Eyewitness*, 1981. She hit the cover of 'Newsweek' after starring opposite a slimy outer-space reptile in *Alien*, 1979. A latter-day Spencer Tracy is what she deserves, and *Half Moon Street*, 1986, has given her at least a chance of finding him.

ABOVE: portrait, 1984

AL PACINO

Pacino's swarthy but sensitive features have a slightly baleful cast redeemed by the soulfulness of his eyes. His characters mirror this intriguing mixture of gentleness and violence, as in *The Godfather* I and II, Coppola's epic in which Pacino played Marlon Brando's avenging son, Michael Corleone, who matures from a taciturn war hero rejecting the Mafia code to the chillingly cold-blooded and isolated head of the family. He showed the same blend of aggression and tenderness in *Serpico*, as the cop with a hippy life-style in Greenwich Village who fights the system his own way, and in *Scarecrow*, 1973, in which he is Gene Hackman's violence-resisting partner who nearly gets beaten to death.

Born in a rough New York neighbourhood and of Sicilian descent, Pacino's parents separated when he was young; brought up by his mother and grandparents, he was rebellious and disturbed at school. He has an affinity for 'outsider' roles, conveying complex, stormy emotions with restraint; the impression is that Pacino has been there himself and doesn't want to talk about it too much. As such, there are elements in the persona that can be traced back to Bogart's defensive introspection in *Casablanca*, and to some of Eastwood's cool, austere, secretive heroes. Interestingly, in *Bobby Deerfield*, 1977, he plays a racing driver whose insecurities are literally hidden behind a defensive covering of helmet, dark glasses and racing overalls. His twitchy, inept bank robber whose crime was committed to finance his boyfriend's sex-change operation in *Dog Day Afternoon*, 1975, and cop hunting down a mass murderer in *Cruising*, 1980, both of whom explored the mores and psychology of sexual ambiguity.

LEFT: publicity portrait for *Scarecrow*, 1973

DUSTIN HOFFMAN

Hoffman is not very handsome, but he is extremely attractive. As a leading man, he is the sexy ingenu still discovering new delights: even now in his late forties, he retains the air of puzzled eroticism and youthful sense of adventure that made him a sex-symbol overnight in *The Graduate*, 1967. Held in thrall by Mrs Robinson, Anne Bancroft, and unable to fulfil his father's expectations, he achieved grace and a happy ending for the film by running off with Mrs Robinson's daughter as she stood at the altar with her awful fiancé her mother had approved for her.

Named after the silents star, Dustin Farnum, by his movie-mad mother,

Hoffman's character can be plotted from his mouth, which still curves up with an expression of gratified surprise, rather than down with the disillusionment of middle-age. It's this gentle quality which made him so ill-at-ease in the violence of *Straw Dogs*, a film which was far more up Pacino's street. Interestingly, several of his characters have involved him in the exploration of his female side: as the emasculated Ratso, mothering boyish, innocent Jon Voight in *Midnight Cowboy*, 1969, the father refusing Meryl Streep her son in *Kramer vs Kramer*, 1979, and the actor who becomes a woman for the sake of his

career, but resolves his personal dilemmas by reasserting his masculinity for love of Jessica Lange in *Tootsie*, 1982. What stops the Hoffman character from comic pathos is the seam of stubborn self-righteousness that lurks beneath his timid charm. He parodied it in the opening moments of *Tootsie*, when he justified to his agent his application of Method acting to the role of a tomato in a children's show.

ABOVE: *Agatha*, 1979

221

KATHLEEN TURNER

Kathleen Turner walked into Lawrence Kasdan's *Body Heat*, 1981, as an unknown, and made the part of the coolly erotic killer her own. Thus she took on the *film noir* ghosts of Barbara Stanwyck and Lauren Bacall and, against all odds, won. Here, everybody thought, was a real find, a *femme fatale* for the eighties. So she surprised even her own admirers when she turned up as a comic vamp opposite Steve Martin in the hilarious *The Man With Two Brains*, 1983; and then turned into a timid young novelist transported into a world of romantic adventure with Michael Douglas for *Romancing the Stone*, 1984. Nobody had anticipated such adaptability. But when *Crimes of Passion*, 1985, was released with Turner as China Blue, a night-time hooker and day-time fashion designer, it suddenly dawned that Turner wasn't just a find, she was an authentic screen actress with a range that was truly staggering. She proved that again in *Prizzi's Honour*, 1985, opposite Jack Nicholson. She effortlessly played out to the limits of black comedy as a devious Mafia hit-girl who conveniently falls in love with the hit-man who has to kill her; the challenge of scoring points off Nicholson was nothing compared to making her character believable. It is not surprising that she should have become a strong contender for the position of Hollywood's most versatile actress, and her follow-up with Michael Douglas in Lewis Teague's *The Jewel of the Nile*, 1986, has only increased her popularity. There hasn't been anybody quite like her for years.

LEFT: publicity portrait for *Body Heat*, 1981

DEBRA WINGER

Admirers of Debra Winger have been known to refer to her as a mythical Jewish American Princess swept up on to the big screen. It has always seemed a dubious compliment, but at least it suggests that the actress who once played Wonder Woman's kid sister on television has now graduated to better things. She has had some career doubts and some false starts, as her spell on a kibbutz and later studying sociology suggest. But having survived television and minor film roles in *Slumber Party '57*, 1976, and *Thank God It's Friday*, 1978, she set her sights on the big time. The first step was snatching the lead opposite John Travolta in *Urban Cowboy*, 1980, in which Winger memorably tamed a mechanical bull in a saloon as if it were second nature. Her moment of true glory came in *An Officer and a Gentleman*, 1982, for her love scenes with Richard Gere helped to make this military fairy-tale somehow believable and an unexpected smash hit; she received her reward with an Oscar nomination. And since no-one talks about her role in *Cannery Row*, 1982, because so few people saw it, it seemed that her second Oscar nomination for *Terms of Endearment*, 1983, followed hard on her first, and she was showered in gold dust. Her performance as a young daughter dying of cancer was one of which Irene Dunne would have been proud, and what audiences could see through a veil of streaming tears they pronounced splendid. Her versatility showed in *Mike's Murder*, 1984, but truly plum roles like her Oscar contenders may be few and far between.

RIGHT: *An Officer and a Gentleman*, 1982

223

ROBERT REDFORD

ABOVE: *The Great Gatsby*, 1974, with Mia Farrow
OPPOSITE: publicity portrait for *The Natural*, 1984

Redford is a bafflingly ambivalent figure, his smile and eyes not quite co-ordinated in their message. On the one hand he can be the lovable, romping good buddy of *Butch Cassidy and the Sundance Kid* and *The Sting*, on the other, detached and honourable observer of the amoralities behind achievement and success – both his own and that of others. Riding along with him in the limousine in *The Candidate*, 1972, we are allowed to share in his disgusted self-knowledge as he intones his election address in tones of

perfect, resonant sincerity but sentences of pure gibberish. As 'Washington Post' investigative reporter Bob Woodward in *All the President's Men*, 1976, he is compelled by an internal sense of revulsion at the actions of others, which compels him to crack open the flawless façade of political lies and expose the emotional and moral defect beneath.

Although Redford's godlike handsomeness suggests all the Yuppie virtues – success, wealth, athletic achievement – he is in fact anti-urban

and honourable in intent, examining the pioneer spirit in *Jeremiah Johnson*, 1972, the treatment of the American Indian in *Tell Them Willie Boy is Here*, 1970, and the conflict of commercial values with ecological ones in *The Electric Horseman*, 1979.

Redford reached Hollywood through a roundabout route, dropping out of college to try out a career as a painter in Europe, then joining the American Academy of Dramatic Arts on his return. His first big screen success came in 1969, with *Butch Cassidy*, but he had been a leading man since taking his Broadway role in the romantic comedy 'Barefoot in the Park' to the screen in 1967.

His exploration of American attitudes to success and winning began in 1969 with *Downhill Racer*, in which he played an unlikable skier obsessed by his desire for a medal to the exclusion of all human requirements; there were similar elements in the aerial stuntman in *The Great Waldo Pepper*, 1975. In those kinds of role, his characters' emotional and sexual needs are negligible, their relationships negotiable, compared with their drive for power.

By the mid-seventies Redford was America's most popular box-office star. Avoiding off-screen publicity, Redford has a wife and three children, campaigns on environmental issues, espouses liberal political causes and spends much of his time in Utah, of which he owns plenty — a ranch, a horse farm, a ski resort and several thousand acres of land.

ABOVE: publicity portrait for *The Way We Were*, 1973
RIGHT: *The Electric Horseman*, 1979, with Jane Fonda

William Hurt can be summed up in one word: *intense*. At the beginning of his film career, he was described by *Time* magazine as 'the WASP movie-idol of the Eighties', but this label now seems inapt and frivolous. Hurt takes his acting seriously and he has discovered the secret of retaining control while immersing himself in roles. He had compiled a solid track record off-Broadway before he landed his first film role, as the obsessed scientist in *Altered States*, 1980. Obsession seems to come naturally to him: he went on to play the caretaker obsessed by Sigourney Weaver's TV journalist in *Eyewitness*, 1981, and the sleazy lawyer who is obsessed – to the point of murder – with Kathleen Turner's *femme fatale* in *Body Heat*, 1981. Next came the wounded drug dealer of *The Big Chill*, 1983, an ensemble piece in which Hurt managed to dominate, quite effortlessly, through the sheer insistence of his underplaying. His performance as the Russian detective in *Gorky Park*, 1983, by comparison, seemed laboured. It was as if he were taking himself rather *too* seriously. But he rallied with a vengeance, winning an Academy Award as the camp homosexual in *Kiss of the Spider Woman*, 1985, and helping Marlee Maitlin to win one as his deaf co-star in *Children of a Lesser God*, 1986.

Even though Hurt has always commanded respect, it was with *Broadcast News*, 1987, that he finally managed to win friends and influence people. As Tom Grunick, the upwardly-mobile television anchor man, he produced a likeable portrait of someone whose shallow charm and slick social know-how should, by rights, have made the audience dislike him intensely.

RIGHT: publicity portrait for *Broadcast News*, 1987.
Photographer Bonnie Schiffman

JESSICA LANGE

Jessica Lange must be the only Hollywood leading lady of recent times who had to look for a comeback after her first film. For *King Kong*, 1976, was so derisibly tacky that despite a seven-year contract to its producer Dino De Laurentiis, Lange did not make another appearance until *All That Jazz*, 1979 – and even then it was in a minor role. She followed that with yet another clinker called *How to Beat the High Cost of Living*, 1980, before finally getting it right with the Lana Turner role of Cora in the remake of *The Postman Always Rings Twice*, 1981, opposite Jack Nicholson. She took full advantage of this peach of a role, displaying

an impetuous sexual yearning which had been noticeably absent in her previous movies. If her performance hinted that she was capable of overstatement, it was nothing compared to her title role as *Frances*, 1982, the sad story of the Hollywood actress Frances Farmer's struggle against mental instability. Lange was nominated for an Oscar for her full-tilt, hysterical portrayal of every last nuance of mental breakdown. It was pure soap opera; but it did push her to the top of the queue for an Oscar, which she won for a comic role opposite Dustin Hoffman's *Tootsie*, also 1982. Her rise to the show business

aristocracy had already been announced by an early association with dancer Mikhail Baryshnikov, and her romance with America's most eligible man, Sam Shepard, only confirmed that status. It also produced a distinguished contribution, *Country*, 1984, to a new cycle of rural movies, even if she is generally more convincing in an urban role with glamorous fringes; and she was superb in – and Oscar nominated for – *Sweet Dreams*, 1985.

ABOVE: *The Postman Always Rings Twice*, 1981, with Jack Nicholson

MIA FARROW

DIANE KEATON

Despite her well-publicized private life – which includes marriages to Frank Sinatra and André Previn, and a romance with Woody Allen – Mia Farrow manages to convince with almost every performance that she is a fresh-faced naïve. Perhaps it is her wide-eyed, freckled face that makes her peculiarly suitable for such epics of urban sinfulness as Roman Polanski's *Rosemary's Baby*, 1968, and *John and Mary*, 1969. She retains her frail charm even when laden down with costume in *The Great Gatsby*, 1974; and in her films with Woody Allen it was decidedly reasserted, from *A Midsummer Night's Sex Comedy*, 1982, through *Zelig*, 1983, to her radiant brilliance in *Broadway Danny Rose*, 1984, *The Purple Rose of Cairo*, 1985, and *Hannah and Her Sisters*, 1986.

BELOW: *The Great Gatsby*, 1974

From playing Woody Allen's favourite kook, to conjuring the heavy emotion of *Shoot the Moon*, 1982, Diane Keaton has, for many, never ceased to be *Annie Hall*, 1977, a role for which she won a Best Actress Oscar. She has a bizarre West Coast vagueness which was the ideal attribute for co-starring opposite the nervy, articulate New Yorker Woody Allen in *Play It Again Sam*, 1972, through to *Manhattan*, 1979. Even so, her dramatic roles in *Interiors*, 1978, *Looking for Mr Goodbar*, 1977, and *Mrs Soffel*, 1984, leave a sense of overpowering vacancy, and if her sincerity in *Reds*, 1981, was clearly under strain, surprisingly nothing has yet managed to dent her personal popularity.

ABOVE: *Interiors*, 1978

BURT REYNOLDS

Energetic and hairy-chested, Burt Reynolds's confidence in his own sexual identity shines through his screen roles whether he is playing as a cop, a footballer or a lovable miscreant. Slightly self-mocking about his footballer physique and private reputation as a virile playboy bachelor, he was the first completely nude male centrefold in 'Cosmopolitan' in 1972 – though it's a decision he has said he regrets.

Born in Georgia, the grandson of a Cherokee Indian, Reynolds was heading for a pro-football career until it was terminated by a car accident. He became a middling star in the late sixties – when he was already moulting at quite a rate – via Westerns, then a major one in John Boorman's *Deliverance*, 1972. In the same year, he dressed up as a nun in *Fuzz*, showing a nice sense of the sexually ridiculous and a flair for hard-edged comedy which has remained his mainstay ever since. *White Lightning*, 1973, introduced the character of Gator, who has appeared in various sequels; in *The Longest Yard*, 1974, he played a convict coaching his fellow inmates for a crunch match against the screws. He played a footballer again in *Semi-Tough*, 1977, stealing Jill Clayburgh from Kris Kristofferson at the end of various louche adventures, and in *Sharky's Machine*, 1981, a demoted cop with an appealing lack of seriousness about busting a crime syndicate with the help of a call-girl ring. Recently, he went through the male menopause in *Starting Over*, and starred in *City Heat*, a romp set in the Prohibition years, with Clint Eastwood.

LEFT: *Sam Whiskey*, 1969

Depardieu calls to mind both Jean Gabin and Jean-Paul Belmondo. Since *Les Valseuses*, 1974, in which he established his rugged, working-class image as a virile petty criminal, he has become one of the biggest sex symbols in European cinema and his status was confirmed when he co-starred with Robert de Niro in *1900*, as a peasant turned partisan-hero.

Depardieu's role in *Les Valseuses* is said to contain many elements of his own childhood. He became attracted to acting while working as a beach-boy in Cannes during the Film Festival, went to Paris to train, then worked his way up through television and the theatre. A forceful presence, Depardieu has often been an off-beat leading man, presented several times as the object of female subversion and rage. In *The Last Woman*, he castrated himself with an electric knife, in *Bye Bye Monkey* he was raped by a feminist theatre group in a ghastly New York some time in the future, and struggled with bewilderment to conquer his girl's depressions only for her to abandon him in favour of a pubescent boy in *Préparez Vos Mouchoirs*. In *The Return of Martin Guerre*, he played the part of a medieval peasant who leaves his village as a callow newly-wed, only to return years later as a supposed war-hero. Welcomed with open arms by the village, his identity is later challenged and he is sentenced to death by the ecclesiastical court, but only after his wife has knowingly abandoned the law, and truth, to plead for him through her love.

ABOVE: *1900*, 1976

GLENN CLOSE

Glenn Close is full of surprises. A doctor's daughter from Connecticut, she began her career with a couple of radical earth mother roles in *The World According to Garp*, 1982, and *The Big Chill*, 1983.

She went on to play female virtue personified in *The Natural*, 1984, inspiring Robert Redford to new heights of baseball brilliance, while in *Jagged Edge*, 1985, she was a credible career woman, overcoming professional scruples to become emotionally entangled with her client, murder suspect Jeff Bridges.

It is hard to believe that only a few years on, Glenn Close was hailed as 'The Most Hated Woman in America' on the strength of her performance in the hugely successful *Fatal Attraction*, 1987. It was her portrayal of the spurned and furious Alex which put her firmly on the map and guaranteed her star status. Up until the point at which Alex ceases to be human and becomes a rampaging bogeywoman, Close turned out a sympathetic portrayal of a woman who feels herself used and abused by the male sex.

It would be a pity if she were to be typecast in similar roles for the rest of her career, because she has already proved herself to be an immensely versatile actress. In *Dangerous Liasons*, 1988, however, she was too open, too honest and too all-American for the character of the scheming French marquise. It looks like the shadow of Alex will be dogging her for a long time to come.

ABOVE: *Jagged Edge*, 1985, with Jeff Bridges

GRETA SCACCHI

Since her native British film industry remains a notorious black hole for aspiring movie actresses, Greta Scacchi has had to cast her net far and wide for good parts. Her impish good looks first attracted attention in James Ivory's Anglo-Indian production *Heat and Dust*, 1983; she plays an English wife who scandalizes her Raj friends by falling in love with an Indian. She surfaced again in *The Coca Cola Kid*, 1985, as an Australian radical opposite American Eric Roberts, in a film directed by the Yugoslav Dusan Makavejev. In between were strong roles on British television opposite Laurence Olivier in 'The Ebony Tower', 1984, and with James Mason and Alan Bates in 'Dr Fischer of Geneva', 1984; a leading role in the Australian television series 'Waterfront', 1983; and the title role of 'Camille', 1984, for American television. The British thriller *Defence of the Realm*, 1985, sadly underplayed her role as a Member of Parliament's secretary who is caught up in a spy scandal, but she survived long enough on screen to demonstrate that she is worthy of more than that. Scacchi is the daughter of an Italian painter and an Englishwoman, and it's been her fate to have to renew her passport and to suffer at the hands of one or two domineering directors and stars; but one day she should at last get her own back.

RIGHT: portrait, 1985.
    Photographer Donald Cooper

EDDIE MURPHY

Eddie Murphy has got what it takes, no question, but will he last? By the time he was twenty years old, he was a successful stand-up comedian and a star of American television's *Saturday Night Live*. Aged twenty-one, he burst on to the big screen in *48 HRS*, 1982. As a snappy-mouthed convict dressed in an Armani suit, he provided the perfect complement to Nick Nolte's dour cop; it remains his best film to date. His disarming grin and unmistakeable laugh (best transcribed as 'Hyuk Hyuk') coupled with sterling support from Dan Aykroyd, helped make *Trading Places*, 1983, a huge success.

Murphy first received solo top-billing as the streetwise Axel Foley in *Beverley Hills Cop*, 1984, a role which had been originally intended for Sylvester Stallone. The film was a box-office smash, but the weaknesses of the formula were shown up in the sequel, which relied too heavily on its star's ability to talk dirty with audacious charm. In *The Golden Child*, 1986, Murphy received his first screen kiss from the chaste lips of Charlotte Lewis, and in *Coming to America*, 1988, he played a naive African prince looking for a bride in New York (a variation on Paul Hogan's *Crocodile Dundee*). *Eddie Murphy Raw*, 1988, his live concert film, suggested that his rapid rise to stardom has left him stranded with the image of a rich and bigoted superstud. But he is still young, and time will tell where he will go from here.

LEFT: publicity portrait for *Trading Places*, 1983.
Photographer Mary Ellen Mark

MICHAEL DOUGLAS

Kirk Douglas is a hard act to follow, but his son is having little trouble in doing so. For a while, Michael Douglas looked as though he had found his niche as a producer, picking up a Best Academy Award for *One Flew Over the Cuckoo's Nest*, 1975, and scoring another smash hit with *The China Syndrome*, 1979. He gave workmanlike acting performances in *The China Syndrome*, as a crusading television cameraman trying to prise open a nuclear cover-up, and in *Coma*, 1978, offering back-up to Genevieve Bujold when she stumbles across a spare-parts surgery racket. As a producer, he struck gold again with *Romancing the Stone*, 1984, and its sequel, *The Jewel of the Nile*, 1985. He also starred in both films, but on the screen he never looked completely at ease as the rollicking adventurer who teams up with Kathleen Turner's prim lady writer.

It was not until *Fatal Attraction*, 1987, that Douglas proved that he could deliver the goods in a leading role. The film was little more than an upmarket monster movie masquerading as adult entertainment, but Douglas held the film together as the family man who commits casual adultery and then watches his life fall apart when his spurned mistress turns into an avenging fury. It was a subtle, shady performance, but in *Wall Street*, 1987, he demonstrated that he could also come out with all guns blazing. The role of Gordon Gekko, the Machiavellian wheeler-dealer, might almost have been written for Michael's father, but Douglas Jr made it his own and fully deserved his Academy Award for Best Actor. With his striped shirts and scarlet braces, his one-liners ('Lunch is for wimps') and his aura of power, Gekko is simultaneously attractive and repulsive: a villain for our times.

RIGHT: publicity portrait for *Wall Street*, 1987.
Photographer Andy Schwartz

CHER

Only a few pop stars have crossed the great divide from vinyl to celluloid with lasting success, but Cher has managed it better than most. Visions of her in Astrakhan-trimmed hippy clothes, crooning 'I got you babe' alongside ex-husband Sonny Bono, now seem like a quaint prelude to a sustained and serious acting career.

It was director Robert Altman who gave Cher her big break by casting her in both the stage and screen versions of *Come Back to the Five and Dime, Jimmy Dean, Jimmy Dean*, 1982, in which she acquitted herself admirably. She was a revelation, however, in *Silkwood*, 1983, as the lesbian girlfriend of doomed Meryl Streep, and stunning in *Mask*, 1985, as the biker's moll who knows that her deformed son is as beautiful on the inside as he is hideous on the outside. In *The Witches of Eastwick*, 1987, she managed to hold her own, just, against the combination of special effects and Jack Nicholson operating at full throttle. But it was *Moonstruck*, 1987, that gave her the role of a lifetime and earned her the Academy Award for Best Actress. As the widow who falls for her fiancé's brother, she blossomed and glowed like an old-style operatic heroine. Only the make-over scene, in which her new hairstyle and flashy outfit were supposed to transform her from a frump into a raging beauty taxed the imagination, since she was attractive enough to begin with. Indeed, Cher is one of the few stars whose real-life image is so outrageously glamorous that she has to tone down her appearance for film roles. In *Suspect*, 1987, she could not subdue the glamour enough to pass muster as an overworked attorney, but her performance was nevertheless that of a *star*.

LEFT: publicity portrait for *Moonstruck*, 1987.

Jeff Bridges comes from a Hollywood acting dynasty. The son of Lloyd Bridges and the brother of Beau Bridges, he is also one of the most underrated film actors of recent times; perhaps because he makes acting look so easy. He does not bother with affected accents, quirky mannerisms, or any of the other devices which tend to win critical praise and reap Academy Awards these days. Instead, he strolls through his films with a complete lack of self-consciousness. His boyish good looks and engaging grin first attracted attention in 1971, in the small-town setting of *The Last Picture Show*.

He went on to appear in some of the best, if not the best-received, American movies of the Seventies: *Bad Company*, 1972, *Fat City*, 1972, *The Last American Hero*, 1973, and *Stay Hungry*, 1976.

In the Eighties, Bridges proved that his easy manner went hand-in-hand with extreme versatility; he played an aimless beach bum caught up in conspiracy and murder in *Cutter's Way*, 1981, a living computer game in *Tron*, 1982, a friendly alien in *Starman*, 1984, and a fall-guy who falls for his best friend's girl in *Against All Odds*, 1984. In *Jagged Edge*, 1985, he managed to

keep the audience guessing until the very last frame with his portrayal of a charming newspaper magnate who might or might not have murdered his wife. He followed this up with the equally ambiguous but rather less charming cop who teams up with a drunken Jane Fonda in *The Morning After*, 1986. In *Tucker*, 1988, he was back in engaging boyish mode as the 1940s car designer who took on the big boys and lost; no one but Bridges could have got away with being so irrepressibly good-natured about it all.

ABOVE: *Jagged Edge*, 1985

KELLY McGILLIS

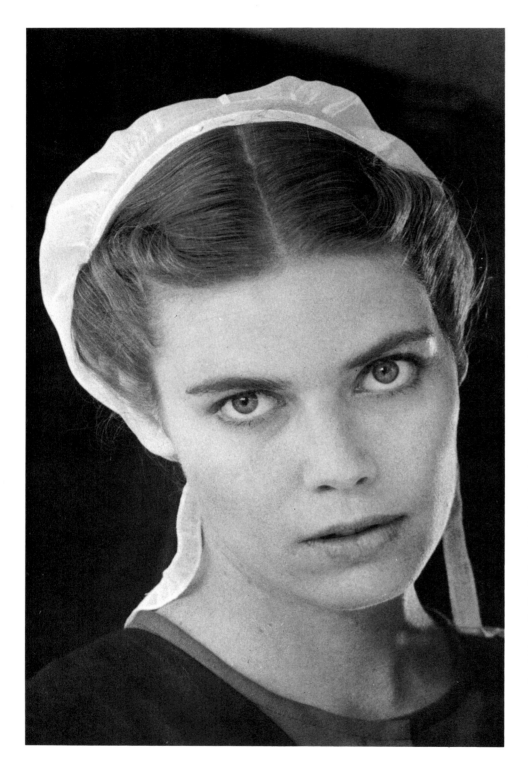

Were it not for the determined set of her jaw and the perpetual hint of puzzled anxiety hovering over her brow, Kelly McGillis might have been in danger of embodying the All-American Girl. But it is those cracks in the veneer which give her a head-start over her blander contemporaries; McGillis really does succeed in persuading you that there is a mind at work behind the pretty face. She was still studying acting at the prestigious Juillard school in New York when she made her film debut in *Reuben, Reuben*, 1983, as the 'strapping girl with rousing breasts and hair like ripe wheat' who bowls over Tom Conti's boozy Scottish poet. But it wasn't until *Witness*, 1985, that moviegoers really began to sit up and take notice. As Rachel Lapp, the young Amish widow who falls for Harrison Ford's big-city cop, she conveyed an intriguing blend of innocence and plucky self-sufficiency which lent her love scenes an added will-she-or-won't-she intensity.

As if to demonstrate her versatility, she then played an aeronautical instructor in the hugely successful *Top Gun*, 1986, although her romance with Tom Cruise took second place to the film's real stars, a fleet of F-14 fighter planes. However, she was the undisputed heroine of *The House on Carroll Street*, 1988, scampering through New York in pursuit of wicked pro-Nazi villains. Her serious side came to the fore in *The Accused*, 1988, where the role as a district attorney assigned to Jodie Foster's rape case gained extra resonance after her courageous admission that she too had once been the victim of a sexual assault.

LEFT: *Witness*, 1985

HARRISON FORD

For an actor who is notoriously reluctant to talk about himself in interviews, Harrison Ford has chosen some curiously high-profile roles. After working as a carpenter to the Hollywood stars, he became a sporadic bit-player for the Movie Brat directors in films such as *American Graffiti*, 1973, and *The Conversation*, 1974. He finally hit the big-time when George Lucas cast him as Han Solo, the wisecracking second-string hero of the *Star Wars* trilogy, 1977-83. But the role which lifted him into the top rank was that of the bullwhip-wielding Indiana Jones in *Raiders of the Lost Ark*, 1981, and its sequels. Had his career stopped there, one might be forgiven for dismissing him as an amiable lightweight, but he has gone on to prove himself an actor of enormous depth and subtlety.

Ford is the natural successor to Gary Cooper, capable of suggesting the moral dilemmas and ambiguities that lie beneath the rugged exterior of the unflappable man of action. As the robot-hunter torn between duty and compassion in *Blade Runner*, 1982, he added a solid human heart to the hi-tech dazzle. He was the tough cop in *Witness*, 1985, trying manfully to suppress his physical instincts when he takes refuge in a peaceful Amish community (and incidentally demonstrating in the barn-building sequence that he had lost none of his carpenty skills). As the protagonist of *The Mosquito Coast*, 1986 he allowed his heroic demeanour to crack wide open as his dreams to build a utopia in Central America drag him down to obsession and madness; one can think of few actors of similar stature who would be prepared to play such an unsympathetic character. And in *Frantic*, 1988, he brought touches of humourous desperation to his portrayal of a bewildered man ensnared by a complex Hitchcockian web.

RIGHT: *Raiders of the Lost Ark*, 1981

INDEX